Elgar: *'Enigma' Variations*

Elgar's Variations for Orchestra, commonly known as the *'Enigma' Variations*, marked an epoch both in his career and in the renaissance of English music at the turn of the century. First performed in 1899 under Hans Richter, the work became his passport to national fame and international success. From the first, listeners have been intrigued by the 'enigma' of the title and the identity of the 'friends pictured within', to whom the work was dedicated. Appearing in the centenary year of the work's completion, this book elucidates what is known and what has been said about the work and the enigma, and directs future listeners to what matters most: the inspired qualities of the music.

CAMBRIDGE MUSIC HANDBOOKS

GENERAL EDITOR Julian Rushton

Recent titles

Elgar: *'Enigma' Variations*

Julian Rushton

West Riding Professor of Music
The University of Leeds

CAMBRIDGE
UNIVERSITY PRESS

PUBLISHED BY THE PRESS SYNDICATE OF THE UNIVERSITY OF CAMBRIDGE
The Pitt Building, Trumpington Street, Cambridge CB2 1RP, United Kingdom

CAMBRIDGE UNIVERSITY PRESS
The Edinburgh Building, Cambridge CB2 2RU, UK   http://www.cup.cam.ac.uk
40 West 20th Street, New York, NY 10011-4211, USA   http://www.cup.org
10 Stamford Road, Oakleigh, Melbourne 3166, Australia

First published 1999

Printed in the United Kingdom at the University Press, Cambridge

Typeset in Ehrhardt MT 10½/13, in QuarkXPress™   [SE]

A catalogue record for this book is available from the British Library

Library of Congress cataloguing in publication data

Rushton, Julian.
Elgar, Enigma variations / Julian Rushton.
p.   cm. – (Cambridge music handbooks)
Includes bibliographical references and index.
ISBN 0 521 63175 0 (hardback). – ISBN 0 521 63637 X (paperback)
1. Elgar, Edward, 1857–1934.   Variations on an original theme.
I. Title.   II. Series.
ML410.E41R87   1998
784.2′1825–dc21   98–22042   CIP

ISBN 0 521 63175 0 hardback
ISBN 0 521 63637 X paperback

(****)

Contents

Introduction

1880 is usually given as the date of the 'modern Renaissance' in English music. For me it began about 20 years later when I first knew Elgar's Enigma Variations. I felt that here was music the like of which had not appeared in this country since Purcell's death. (Gustav Holst)[1]

The title of the work which is my subject corresponds only informally to the title of this handbook. Undoubtedly we shall go on calling Elgar's Op. 36 *'Enigma' Variations*, as does the cover of the *Elgar Complete Edition*.[2] But the autograph title-page reads only 'Variations for Orchestra composed by Edward Elgar Op. 36'.[3] Above the theme itself the word 'Enigma' appears, in the hand of A. J. Jaeger ('Nimrod'), added presumably at Elgar's request when publication was under way at Novello's.[4] This was not only Elgar's first international success, but also his first work to be published in full score; then it was entitled 'Variations on an Original Theme'.

On this reading 'Enigma' is not the title of the composition, but an emblem for the theme – perhaps only for its first few bars; in 1899 Elgar referred to the appearance of 'the principal motive (Enigma)' at a point in the finale, marked *grandioso* (cue 68) where the melody is derived only from bars 1–4.[5] On publication, however, 'Enigma' appears centred beneath VARIATIONS, implying a stronger connection between the word and the whole work.[6] There is no reason why an autograph score should be privileged over a published score acknowledged by the composer. To what, then, does 'Enigma' really apply? In order not to prejudice the matter, I shall refer to the composition as a whole as *'Variations'* or 'Op. 36', and confine the word 'enigma' to discussion of the theme and the enigma itself. Individual variations are designated either by number (Roman numerals, as in the score) or by their heading, usually a set of initials. To clarify these references, table I.1 lists the sections into which

1

Table I.1. *The movements of the Variations Op. 36*

Variation number	Heading	Interpretation	Cue (first bar of each variation)	Bars	Ends fermata or *attacca*
Theme	Enigma			1–17	bars 18–19 are a link
I	(C.A.E.)	Caroline Alice Elgar, the composer's wife	2	20–40	fermata
II	(H.D.S-P.)	Hew David Steuart-Powell, amateur pianist	5	41–96	fermata
III	(R.B.T.)	Richard Baxter Townshend, scholar, author, eccentric	8	97–131	fermata
IV	(W.M.B.)	William Meath Baker, 'squire' of Hasfield Court	11	132–163	fermata
V	(R.P.A.)	Richard Penrose Arnold, son of Matthew Arnold	15	164–187	*attacca*
VI	(Ysobel)	Isabel Fitton, amateur viola player	19	188–209	fermata
VII	(Troyte)	Arthur Troyte Griffith, artist and architect	23	210–280	fermata
VIII	(W.N.)	Winifred Norbury, secretary, Worcestershire Philharmonic Society	30	281–307	*attacca*
IX	(Nimrod)	August Johannes Jaeger, of Novello's	33	308–350	fermata
X	(Dorabella) Intermezzo	Dora Penny (later Mrs Richard Powell)	38	351–424	fermata
XI	(G.R.S.)	George Robertson Sinclair, organist at Hereford, owner of Dan, a bulldog	47	425–464	fermata
XII	(B.G.N.)	Basil Nevinson, amateur cellist	52	465–492	*attacca*
XIII	(***) Romanza	Lady Mary Lygon (later Trefusis), of Madresfield Court	55	493–543	fermata
XIV	(E.D.U.) Finale	Edu=Elgar himself	61 (to 83)	544–780	fine

Op. 36 is divided, with the rehearsal cues which are in every score, and the bar numbers which are included only in the *Complete Edition*. In discussion, since the *Complete Edition* will not be in many private libraries, I use the rehearsal cues and indicate bars by the form cue: bar after cue (e.g. 55:4 means the fourth bar after cue 55).

All scores of *Variations* are based photographically on the full score published by Novello's in 1900 and reprinted as a miniature score by Novello's, and later as Eulenburg Miniature Score No. 884; this was reissued with a new introduction by Esther Cavett-Dunsby in 1985. The *Complete Edition* produced a full score the following year, in which the text was scrutinised and corrected; this has an important foreword (including a valuable account of the publication history) and critical notes.[7] The only authorised variants are between versions with alternative instrumentation, such as solo piano (by the composer) or two pianos; while they may appear anachronistic in an age of recording, such skilful transcriptions offer great enjoyment.

Elgar's Op. 36 stands at the portal of our perception of English symphonism. Yet this is no symphony, and it was preceded by other orchestral works by British composers, including several distinctive symphonies and programmatic works (by Potter, Pierson, Macfarren, Sullivan, Parry, Stanford, and Wallace, not to mention Elgar himself), as well as other sets of variations (see chapter 2). But as Holst noticed in the 1920s (see epigraph), *Variations* continued, and continues as it enters its second century, to occupy a special place in our perception. It marked the coming to pre-eminence of the forty-one-year-old composer whose first symphony was later proclaimed by the German conductor Hans Richter as 'the greatest symphony of modern times, written by the greatest composer'.[8] It was Richter who brought *Variations* before the public, and launched Elgar onto the series of orchestral works (marches, symphonies, concertos, overtures, and *Falstaff*) which lie at the heart of his achievement.

Composers commonly go out of fashion shortly after their death; Elgar achieved this in his lifetime, F. H. Shera, for instance, referring in 1931 to 'today's lack of admiration'.[9] Despite a resurgence of activity in the later 1920s, when he produced some lesser works and recorded greater ones, Elgar was alienated from the post-war world and manifestations of modernism. In his influential 'study of music in decline', Constant Lambert made it clear that, even while alive, Elgar was seen as a prelapsarian phenomenon at best, and at worst the singer of outmoded kingdom and empire, an Edwardian in a Georgian age.[10] With his developing European success broken by the First World War, Elgar's reputation, even in other Anglophone nations, has never matched his standing in Britain, which has revived markedly since 1950. His music never lost his grip on the home repertory; there were always performances, his marches entered national consciousness along with 'Nimrod', and the first complete recording of *The Dream of Gerontius* was a war-time project.[11] Yet even now much of his output remains in desuetude, notably the smaller vocal works. Elgar was an inspired miniaturist; and gathering short, self-contained musical characterisations into a coherent whole is the essential principle of *Variations*.

No published study of Elgar pre-dates Op. 36; essays and small books appeared from 1900 until shortly before the composer's death, when Basil Maine published a full-length 'life and works'. There followed memorial tributes by those who knew him (notably books by W. H. Reed and Mrs Richard Powell), while other memories remained in manuscript or emanated from relatives and descendants of his friends. The increase in performances was naturally accompanied by critical and scholarly reassessment. In the 1950s new studies of the life and works appeared from Percy M. Young and Diana McVeagh; Michael Kennedy's *Portrait of Elgar* (1968) deepened our understanding of the composer's psychology; further large-scale biographies, steeped in the music, have appeared from Jerrold Northrop Moore and Robert Anderson (see the bibliography).

More specialised literature has developed alongside such major works of synthesis; naturally it is mostly in English, and by British authors. Material is continually being made public, including letters, studies of sketches and compositional methods, bibliographies, and volumes of collected essays. The *Elgar Society Journal*, besides reviews and information, publishes material of biographical interest, which with Elgar may often have a direct bearing on the music. The *Complete Edition*, suspended at the time of writing, promises a monument worthy of Elgar as a composer of canonical status. Two essay collections edited by Raymond Monk contain more specialised studies, and the periodical literature contains signs that critics are at last venturing on analysis and

4

critical appraisal of a depth which with some composers we would take for granted. Naturally, a subliterature is devoted to 'Elgar's Enigma'; indeed, a disproportionate amount of energy has been expended on this hardy perennial of a puzzle at the expense of musical values. Chapter 5 offers some analysis of 'solutions' rather than a new one. Elgar cannot have regarded the alleged enigma as an integral part of his communication to the listening public. He presented the initials of 'friends pictured within', not to disguise their identities but to avoid pointlessly revealing them to the huge majority of contemporary (never mind subsequent) audiences to whom they were complete strangers. Information about the friends is considered and assessed for its musical pertinence in chapter 3.

To many friends not depicted within I offer sincere thanks for their support. Most especially I am indebted to Michael Kennedy, who surveyed the typescript with a sharp eye for detail, historical and editorial, and Brian Trowell, who shared many enigmatic thoughts. Christopher Polyblank and Jeremy Dibble also read sections of the script and loaned unpublished material. My thanks also to Chris Banks of the British Library; Geoffrey Poole; Edward Rushton; Professor Roy Holland who tried vainly to convince me of the virtues of 'Pop goes the weasel' as a 'solution'; (****); Mark Marrington who prepared the music examples; and Penny Souster at Cambridge University Press, without whose friendly encouragement I might never have ventured to write on something which the world may yet say is 'not my subject'. The portrait on the cover is the property of the Elgar Birthplace Museum and is reproduced by kind permission. All music examples drawn from the score of Elgar's *Variations* are reproduced by kind permission of Novello and Co., Ltd.

1

Composition

Elgar before *Variations*

Elgar's output prior to Op. 36 was already varied in conception, scale, and purpose. The choral masterpieces that followed *Variations* – *The Dream of Gerontius*, *The Apostles*, *The Kingdom*, and *The Music Makers* – still tend to overshadow earlier choral works; yet by 1898, at forty-one, Elgar could boast considerable artistic (if not commercial) success, with *The Black Knight* (1892), *Scenes from the Bavarian Highlands* (1895), *The Light of Life* (1896), and *King Olaf* (1896). There were already voices suggesting that this was the best English music since Purcell, and Parry, himself the most firmly established composer in the field, called Elgar (with only a little hindsight) 'a new light of exceptional brilliancy' (other senior composers, Stanford, Mackenzie, and Cowen, were also early admirers).[1] Elgar had written no orchestral music of comparable sophistication. The precursors of *Variations* were light orchestral pieces of inimitable charm, like the string serenade; exquisite salon music, like *Salut d'amour* or *Chanson de nuit*; and minor excursions into exoticism, like *Sérénade Mauresque*. Many ideas of orchestral potential, lying unused in notebooks, happily resurfaced in later compositions, even in Op. 36 itself. The exception is the concert overture of 1890, a broadly conceived and thematically prolific sonata form which takes its mood, rather than any programme, from Froissart's *Chronicles*. *Froissart* matches, or excels, the finest British orchestral output of its time; yet by comparison with Elgar's later symphonic work it seems structurally loose. Despite *The Black Knight*, a fascinating choral symphony on a very different model from precursors like Beethoven's Ninth or Berlioz's *Roméo et Juliette*, Elgar attained his finest symphonic manner only in the finale of Op. 36. The actual variations belong to another world, showing an Elgar by no means exclusively Germanic in orientation, but equally indebted to French composers such as Delibes and Massenet. The discipline of variation form enabled him to harness this gift 'for composing light, witty, and melodious vignettes, which reached an apotheosis in the *Enigma Variations*'.[2]

In 1897 we catch a tantalising glimpse of a conception which may have merged with that of Op. 36. On 19 September Elgar wrote to Nicholas Kilburn:

> Can you tell me where I can find the lines 'Merrily sung the monks of Ely when Knut king rowed by &c.' *as originally written*. They are quoted in Green's History (Short Histy of the English people) & I am writing (perhaps a series) of illustrative movements for orchestra with 'mottoes' – whereof this is one – the simple words have always charmed me & I have done most of the music.[3]

The mottoes were literary and do not imply a theme with variations; but the concept of a series of pieces illustrative of persons is suggestive. Most tantalising are the words 'I have done most of the music'. What became of it? There is no evidence that it was used in Op. 36.[4] Elgar's immediate interest in English history emerged with greater specificity in his next choral project, *Caractacus*, produced at the Leeds Festival on Wednesday 5 October 1898.

In 1897 a group of energetic amateurs founded the Worcestershire Philharmonic Society, an orchestral and choral society designed for Elgar to conduct, which he did with mixed success; the first concert was on 7 May 1898. Elgar had originally offered Leeds an orchestral work, and was depressed when neither they nor Novello's were interested; hence when late in October 1898, after the premiere of *Caractacus*, Elgar conceived a symphony in honour of General Gordon of Khartoum, who had died the death of an Imperial hero thirteen years before, he offered it to the Worcestershire Philharmonic for 1899. When this idea was abandoned, some of its thematic material went into *Gerontius*, but the concept, probably, lingered in his mind another ten years to emerge as Symphony No. 2.[5] In the meantime, however, he had finished *Variations*.

Friends pictured within

The friends who became variations are neither a complete nor a balanced selection from the Elgars' circle at that period. They did not necessarily

7

figure strongly in the composer's past or future and, contrary to what is suggested in Frederick Ashton's ballet, they never took tea together.[6] The composer and his wife can hardly be included in 'friends pictured within', reducing them to twelve. Some were particularly associated with the Elgars' home circle; only a few were musicians with whom the composer was professionally associated.

Among the men, one stands out for the intimacy of his relationship to Elgar the musician. This was A. J. Jaeger, dubbed 'Nimrod' after the biblical 'mighty hunter', whose employment as publishing manager at Novello's brought him into continual contact with the composer.[7] Jaeger dealt with practical issues of publication; he was the principal recipient of letters in which Elgar revealed his cyclical depression, and declared that he would be done with music. Besides making many small suggestions, Jaeger twice insisted on major revisions which markedly enhanced the climaxes of the compositions concerned, *Variations* and *The Dream of Gerontius*. His sensitivity to the composer's moods and his conviction of Elgar's genius probably mattered, over a decade, nearly as much as the support of Alice Elgar herself. The other men, at first glance, are a miscellaneous bunch: minor gentry, professional men who were amateur musicians, an architect, and a cathedral organist, all of whom owe their immortality mainly to Elgar.

The attention of biographers of a heterosexual male turns naturally to the women.[8] Two close friends of the Elgars in the late 1890s wrote memoirs. Dora Penny ('Dorabella'), later Mrs Richard Powell, was an intimate of the household, quite possibly (which she does not claim) because Elgar found her attractive.[9] But Dora was also a friend of Alice, and her relationship to the far older couple seems more filial than amorous. Elgar's acquaintance with Isabel Fitton ('Ysobel') and Winifred Norbury (W.N.) was contingent on the social and musical life of the area; it appears from the sketches that they presented themselves as suitable for variations rather late in the compositional process. The last female portrait is variation XIII, '(***)'. An early list of variations among the sketches (see p. 14) gives the incipit of XIII and marks it as finished; it is given the initial L. Other sketches refer to 'LML', making clear that the dedicatee is Lady Mary Lygon, of Madresfield Court, whom Elgar knew well through her musical activities (including committee work for the Worcestershire Philharmonic). She is, however, the only aristocrat on the list; Elgar was acutely conscious of class, and his father, as piano tuner, used the tradesmen's entrance at Madresfield. Modern scholars, wondering not unreasonably why L.M.L. did not appear in the published score, have questioned whether Lady Mary is really intended; XIII may covertly refer to someone quite different (see chapters 3 and 5).

Friends not pictured within

It was never Elgar's intention to picture his social world with any completeness or collective significance. He was part of a large family, with whom he was on good terms, but his own relations are excluded. His circle of friends and acquaintances was already wide, including groups in the Worcester and Hereford region, in London, and elsewhere. It appears that other friends were at one time intended for inclusion; still more were never considered. Even within the locality, from which the majority is drawn, the selection of friends is patchy.[10] He did not include his boyhood friend Hubert Leicester, flute player and later mayor of Worcester, with whom he remained on good terms for a lifetime and who with Troyte Griffith saw him into his grave at Malvern. The librettist H. A. Acworth is not included although he lived in Malvern and was in Elgar's thoughts in the aftermath of *Caractacus*.[11] Among professional musicians, only the cathedral organist of Hereford (G. R. Sinclair) was represented. A variation was intended for his former assistant Ivor Atkins, since 1897 organist of Worcester, with whom Elgar's musical friendship was closer. Sinclair may have owed his advantage to his bulldog Dan (see chapter 3). The march *Pomp and Circumstance* No. 3 was later dedicated to Atkins.[12]

The reminiscences of Rosa Burley are more revealing than Mrs Powell's amiable *Memories*. Burley was close to the Elgars for many years, initially as headmistress of the Mount School where Elgar taught violin; her memoirs hardly disguise the implication that Elgar was sexually attracted to her. When asked whether she was a variation, she replied 'I am the theme', a joke which may have had a sting.[13] Burley among others demonstrated friendship in a practical way, shortly before the inception of *Variations*, by travelling north for *Caractacus*. Also present were Ivor Atkins, Miss Hyde (fellow-secretary with W.N. of the Worcestershire Philharmonic Society), B.G.N., H.D.S-P., G.R.S., and Lady Mary Lygon. Burley observed that Elgar 'rushed back to Malvern with the air of one who has fought – and is inclined to think he has lost – a heavy engagement'; in fact, however, the Elgars remained in Leeds until the weekend and returned to Malvern via London only on 19 October.[14]

Beyond the Worcester–Hereford region, there is no variation for Elgar's close friend and correspondent Dr Charles Buck of Giggleswick.[15] Perhaps another cellist alongside B.G.N. might have been difficult to accommodate; but Buck was also, and perhaps awkwardly, his confidant in the matter of his broken engagement with Helen Weaver (see chapter 5). Buck and Leicester were perhaps excluded because they were friends of Elgar long before his marriage, of which Op. 36 is partly a celebration; B.G.N. and H.D.S-P. were at Oxford with R.P.A. and Parry, and knew Alice Roberts before she married Elgar in 1889. Mrs Fitton, mother of 'Ysobel', was also close to Alice.[16] For that reason, perhaps, as well as for disguise, Elgar wrote E.D.U. on the finale, rather than his semi-public monogram E.E.; Edu was Alice's pet name for him. Another friend in the North of England, a musician and one of Elgar's principal musical confidants over many years, was Nicholas Kilburn. His variation was planned and conceivably jettisoned out of pique following a letter, a month after the conception of *Variations*, in which Kilburn expressed reservations about *Caractacus*.[17] Kilburn was forgiven and compensated by the dedication of *The Music Makers*, in which Op. 36 is extensively quoted.

Besides Atkins and Kilburn, Sullivan and Parry, eminent composers who had shown kindness to Elgar, were allegedly intended for inclusion. No trace of them exists in the sketches; mercifully, Elgar resisted the temptation of musical parody.[18] Otherwise the selection may result quite simply from the nature of the material; Elgar knew many fine musicians and had other loyal friends, but if we believe the tales attached to the variations, we may wonder whether their personalities lacked musically suggestive quirks. This, at least, may be inferred from 'Dorabella' when, in 1946, she wrote a supplement to her *Memories*: 'The friends were chosen, not because he had any particularly great regard for each one, but because the thought of them gave him ideas which could be described in music.'[19]

Genesis

The story of Op. 36, as often told, is based on Elgar's own accounts, published in his lifetime.[20] Numbers refer to discussion below the familiar texts. (1) On 21 October 1898, after teaching violin all day, Elgar returned exhausted. (2) Soothed by a cigar, he improvised on the piano. (3) Alice, listening with care

> interrupted by saying: 'Edward, that's a good tune.' I awoke from the dream. 'Eh! tune, what tune!' and she said, 'Play it again, I like that tune.' I played and strummed, and played, and then she exclaimed, 'That's the tune.' And that tune is the theme of the Variations.

According to another account, 'The voice of C.A.E. asked with a sound of approval, "What is that?"' (4) Elgar responded to his wife's question 'What is that?' with 'Nothing – but something might be made of it.' He took the initiative and dressed the tune up in various ways, first indicating whose mannerisms he was imitating: 'Powell would have done this (variation 2) or Nevinson would have looked at it like this (variation 12).'[21] Then (5) he challenges her:

> It pleased me, too, and so I went on playing. Stopping short in my tracks, I turned round: 'Whom does that remind you of?' – 'Why', said she, quick as lightning, 'that's Billy Baker going out of the room.'[22]

This last process was repeated with other listeners, including Dora Penny, who was 'in', and Rosa Burley, who was not. (6) Alice encourages Elgar, saying that this conception is surely new.

(1) It may be significant that the improvisation was on what Elgar insisted was his second instrument. Improvisation at the piano was a normal precompositional activity, as was trying out before sympathetic friends sections of music so far unwritten, or written in sketches unintelligible to anyone else.[23] He could nevertheless have been imagining a theme to be played on violins.

(2) Maybe Elgar did indeed hit on the theme, there and then, plus some of the early variation ideas. The belief that we can locate a day for the conception of the major turning-point in Elgar's fortunes is undeniably seductive. The date is significant, also, for those whose theory of the 'enigma' depends upon specific musical associations (see chapter 5). Nevertheless, I would risk suggesting that the theme is not an obvious outcome of pianistic doodling, and may have been in his head for some time. In common with other artists he may quite unconsciously have adapted memories, such as his

improvisation on that day, so that they could be interpreted in a romantically appealing light.

(3) Alice Elgar's musical percipience should not be underestimated. Elgar may have turned to other females for entertainment, even for love, but his love for Alice was coupled with respect for her artistic sensibility. He valued her opinion; without her intervention the piece might have faded away with the Gordon symphony.

(4) Alice's insistence that he retain hold of the shape of the theme will have acted as a stimulus. It is only an assumption that the idea he was using in his improvisation was presented in a manner similar to the eventual theme, although the sketch which followed, probably very quickly, is full and final. The teasing quality of Elgar's response is characteristic; it allegedly led to the conception of H.D.S-P. and B.G.N., friends who had come to Leeds for *Caractacus*. The sketches suggest that these were indeed among the earliest variations to reach something like a definitive form (see below).

(5) Elgar takes the game a stage further. He had recently stayed at the homes of William Baker (W.M.B.) and Richard Arnold (R.P.A.); on sketch evidence, W.M.B., though not R.P.A., was also finished relatively early. Baker liked to organise his guests, and once slammed the door on leaving the room; this was the allusion Alice picked up.

(6) Alice was historically incorrect if she meant that no previous composer had attempted musical portraiture; there are examples by two composers dear to Elgar, Mozart (the slow movement of the piano sonata K. 309) and Schumann (see chapter 2), while Tchaikovsky composed a multifaceted portrait of Nikolay Rubinstein in the Variation movement of his piano trio. Elgar may have been less impressed by the perceived novelty of the idea than by the encouragement to give in to his desire to write orchestral music, in a form less demanding on himself and on audiences than a patriotic and programmatic symphony.

Composition

Despite having initiated Op. 36, Elgar continued to toy with *Gordon* for some time after 21 October. He found the idea of the symphony daunting; on 20 October he had written crossly to Jaeger: 'I like this idee [*sic*] but my dear man *why* should I try??'[24] But, mercurial as ever, he wrote on 'Enigma day' itself, 21 October, to Edwards of *The Musical Times*: '"Gordon" simmereth mighty pleasantly in my (brain) pan & will no doubt boil over one day.'[25] His objections were more economic than artistic, and starting *Variations* did not make him abandon the idea. Yet as early as Monday 24 October, after a busy weekend of improvisation and sketching, the variations had matured enough for Elgar to reveal his plans to Jaeger, couched in his idiosyncratic, teasing English.

> Since I've been back I have sketched a set of Variations (orkestry) on an original theme: the Variations have amused me because I've labelled 'em with the nicknames of my particular friends – *you* are Nimrod. That is to say I've written the variations each one to represent the mood of the 'party' – I've liked to imagine the 'party' writing the var: him (or her) self & have written what I think *they* wd. have written – if they were asses enough to compose – it's a quaint idee & the result is amusing to those behind the scenes & won't affect the hearer who 'nose nuffin'. What think you?

Yet on 11 November, visiting Birchwood in the autumnal fog, he writes only 'The Variations go on slowly but I shall finish 'em some day' and harks back to *Gordon*: 'the thing possesses me, but I can't write it down yet'. Meanwhile, he was doing hack work: orchestrating a comic opera, and answering queries from the publisher on *The Light of Life*, *King Olaf*, and *Froissart*, as well as *Caractacus*. None of this indicates a lack of worldly involvement, or even success, except from the purely financial point of view. His mood, at least as reflected in letters to 'Nimrod', swung manically. On 17 December he is 'sick at heart over music – the whole future seems so hopeless', but on 5 January, in a postscript: 'I say – those variations I like 'em.'[26]

The sketches

For the most part, the sketches show the jotting down and working out of ideas with which the final version has made us familiar. Individual sketches are not dated, and the largest collection, in the British Library, is not only incomplete (there being other sketches in the Elgar Birthplace Museum) but is itself not bound in order.[27] Precise details of Elgar's progress cannot be confirmed by this evidence alone, but there

Table 1.1. *The first list of variations*

1	2 Marking on incipit	3 Elgar's comment	4 Comment
	Theme	[none]	
D[orabella]	Allegr[o]	finished [pencil]	X
Nimrod	Andantin[o]	[none]	IX; bars 1–2 accurate
Troyte	Presto	finished [pencil]	VII
C.A.E.	?come prima	[none]	I; but not final version
[H.D.] S-P.	Allegretto	finished [pencil]	II; two bars ink, third pencil
L[ygon]	[no tempo, but full incipit]	finished [ink]	XIII; only one bar
W.M.B.	Presto strepitiss	finished [ink]	IV
B.G.N.	slow cello solo [pencil]	finished [pencil]	XII
R.P.A.	C min and 12/8 [pencil: no music notation]	[none]	V
I.A./R.B.T.	Scherz[o]	finished [ink]	III; three bars
Kilburn	4/4 [otherwise no notation]	[none]	Not included
G.R.S.	[No notation]	[none]	Page break
W.N.	[two-bar sketch, ink]	[none]	VIII
G.R.S. [again]	Presto [first five notes, pencil]	finished good [pencil]	XI

are other indications of the order of composition. Burley says she first heard C.A.E. and H.D.S-P.; the latter (sketches, folio 2) was certainly drafted early. Elgar marked his early progress by a list of variations, several with musical incipits (see table 1.1), which must have originated fairly early in the compositional process; this marks as finished 'Dorabella', 'Troyte', W.M.B., B.G.N., H.D.S-P., R.B.T., and L. (XIII or (***)), but not C.A.E.[28] 'Dorabella' was apparently conceived before Elgar met its subject, as an intermezzo in an unrealised project, a suite in G for strings.[29] Bracketed additions in columns 1–3 are mine, as is column 4.

After the blank line 'Kilburn' are the words 'next p[age]', but G.R.S. is added at the bottom of this page, below the staves, without any musical notation. The last two entries appear on folio 10. Since the list was first drawn up using ink, the implication is that sections marked 'finished' in ink were completed already; 'finished' in pencil implies later completion. 'Dorabella' dated her visit 1 November, and says she heard R.B.T., W.M.B., 'Troyte', and herself; she also refers to C.A.E. and 'Nimrod'.[30] It need not follow that the list was made earlier than 1 November. The sketches do make clear that C.A.E. was conceived early, but with the melody in a simpler form; its rich texture was a comparatively late invention (see p. 35). The late arrival on the scene of G.R.S. and W.N. could be significant from the point of view of the 'enigma' (see chapter 5). But the most intriguing point about this list concerns the eventual variation III. Ivor Atkins was closer to Elgar than was R. B. Townshend. The musical incipit is in ink; 'I.A.' is written, and heavily deleted, in ink; and 'R.B.T.' is written in pencil, over the musical incipit, whereas all other initials are in the margin. Is it possible that the actual music, here called 'scherzo' (a title missing in the final score), was not conceived with R.B.T. in mind, but with Atkins?

Completion

Scoring, which Elgar usually accomplished at speed with Alice preparing the pages, was begun on 5 February 1899 and finished in two weeks.[31] He then worked on a piano version, more likely to attract Novello's than a full score, suggesting also that 'Dorabella' 'shd. do very well as a separate venture'.[32] Conception and completion were remarkably rapid for Elgar, if he really had no intimation of the work before 21 October 1898. On 21 February 1899 he sent the music to Vert, Hans Richter's London agent, rightly surmising that if Richter performed the piece Novello's (and other conductors and promoters) would take an interest in it. Parry, approached by Jaeger, seems to have lent his support, but the decision to go ahead with a performance was Richter's.[33] Elgar's courageous gesture indicates his clear understanding of the musical value of what he had done – and the relevant value is strictly musical: Richter, certainly, knew 'nuffin' of the programme which had brought the music into existence. Thus it was that Op. 36 cleared a second hurdle: Richter conducted it in London at St James's Hall on 19 June 1899.

The immediate triumph of *Variations* is reflected in Novello's house magazine, *The Musical Times*, in an issue which also contained a profile of Richter.[34] It is curious to find among the tributes a discordant note from 'Nimrod', of all people; undoubtedly moved by his own variation, Jaeger never let his critical faculty sleep, and he protested that the work ended too abruptly. Riled when Jaeger reminded him that Richter was also in favour of a revision, Elgar resisted vigorously: '[27 June] I waited until I had thought it out & now decide that the end is good enough for me . . . . . . You won't frighten me into writing a logically developed movement where I don't want one by quoting other people!'; '[30 June] As to that finale – its [*sic*] most good of you to be interested & I like to have your opinion . . . Now look here the movement was designed to be concise – here's the difficulty of lengthening it – I *could* go on with those themes for ½ a day, but the *key* G is exhausted – the principal motive (Enigma) comes in grandioso [cue 68] on p. 35 in the tonic & it *won't do* to bring it in again: had I intended to make an extended movemt. this wd. have been in some related Key reserving the tonic for the final smash.'[35]

Nevertheless, on 7 July he promised a sketch and on 12 July he acknowledged Jaeger's approval of the addition, which enlarges the work from 684 to 780 bars and requires the addition of an organ. In the score Elgar wrote 'Great is the art of beginning, but greater the art is of ending.'[36]

At the time of the first performance Elgar muddied the interpretative waters by including the word 'Enigma' in his public programme, where he also indicated his friends by their initials; the programme note spoke for the first time of the enigma as such, and throws out clues, or maybe dust in our eyes, with its reference to a 'dark saying' and to 'another and larger theme' (see chapter 5). It has been suggested that he expected his enigma to be rumbled immediately and then forgotten; when it was not, he became disinclined to say anything. Probably the existence of an enigma, and certainly its use as a title, have done the work no harm. Certainly Op. 36 confirmed Elgar's growing reputation at home. The second performance, in New Brighton (July) under Bantock, was the last with the original finale. Elgar conducted the premiere with new finale at the Three Choirs Festival (Worcester) in September, shortly before the premiere of *Sea Pictures* in Norwich. Richter played it in London the following month, with Dohnányi playing his own piano concerto and in the presence of Vaughan Williams; in February 1900 Richter took it north (Birmingham, Liverpool, Manchester, and Bradford).[37]

Ironically, success led to a widening of the Elgars' circle of friends, many of whom (Rodewald, Schuster, Worthington, Stuart-Wortley) drive the Op. 36 friends from the pages of biographies covering the following decades. These were people who recognised the unique value of Elgar through hearing *Variations* and *The Dream of Gerontius* which followed in 1900. Musicians were in no doubt where the breakthrough came: Parry, equivocal about *Caractacus*, called *Variations* 'Quite brilliantly clever and genuine orchestral music' and wrote cordially to the composer.[38] From being, at its inception, a domestic game, *Variations* became Elgar's most approachable larger work, and the most frequently performed, even when his reputation was in decline. And it has always been recognised as a defining moment not only in Elgar's career, but in the development of British music. Reviewing a later period, Stephen Banfield identified at the end of each World War 'stylistic *loci* in the reassertion of British music following its lean period in the nineteenth century', Holst's *The Planets* and Britten's *Peter Grimes*.[39] But the first such *locus* was Elgar's *Variations*.

2

Variations: the theme

Precedents

The orchestral variation set was a well-established genre before Elgar, and Op. 36 is part of a remarkable surge of interest in this form in Britain at the end of the nineteenth century.[1] Orchestral variations, unlike those for solo instruments, are seldom merely ornamental. They diverge, therefore, from the virtuosic type of variation, which mostly overlays the theme with an encrustation of jewellery. The virtuoso type is not necessarily shallow; sets of studies in the form of variations composed by Beethoven (the C minor variations, WoO 80) and Brahms (the *Paganini* variations, Op. 35) combine virtuosity with strictness to attain the peculiar musical power which resides only in the utmost abstraction from extramusical considerations. Ornamental techniques are naturally used for concertante variations, such as Tchaikovsky's *Variations on a Rococo Theme* for cello and orchestra (1876) or Franck's *Symphonic Variations* (1885), which are more than merely diverting.

In the nineteenth century, genres have a happy way of overlapping, resulting at best not in confusion but in richness. Orchestral sets of variations without a soloist are often designated 'symphonic': such variations translate the spirit of strict, nonvirtuosic, and usually abstract, variation patterns to the symphony orchestra, and aspire to match the symphony in energy, seriousness, and the prestige of being heard as a concert item, a context of edification as of entertainment. Variation form lends itself particularly well to an utterance directed at a public whose musical education and concentration might not match its enthusiasm, for it provides the listener with repeated points of melodic and structural reference.

Before Elgar, the most significant example by an English composer was *Symphonic Variations* (on an original theme) by Parry, composed for

18

the Philharmonic Society in 1897.[2] To use an original theme was comparatively rare, perhaps because the obvious models in the orchestral repertory were Brahms's *Variations on a Theme of Haydn* Op. 56 (1873) and Dvořák's *Symphonic Variations* Op. 78 (1877), based on a Czech folk-song. Orchestral variations by Stanford (with solo piano, 1898), Wood, Gatty, and Hurlstone (all 1899), and by Coleridge-Taylor and Delius, all make use of traditional melodies.[3] The choice of a traditional theme imposes restraints, if only as a courtesy to the material, particularly if the theme is taken from an earlier composer. When a traditional theme is used, its contribution to the new art-work may include the delight of recognition when it emerges, from time to time, from the colourful and ingenious derivations the composer contrives, as for example in Dohnányi's *Variations on a Nursery Song* (1914). Dependence on pre-existing music implies a certain objectivity and again reflects the common practice of using variations for display of virtuoso (including solo and orchestral) technique; the genre is not always associated with intimate feeling although, under Elgar's influence, Bantock composed his *Helena* variations on original theme (1899), which 'picture' his wife.[4]

Whether or not we use the unofficial title 'Enigma', we might still consider Op. 36 mistitled 'Variations for Orchestra', since it hardly conforms to the organic, teleological ideal of 'symphonic' variations. Ostensibly a theme with fourteen variations, the set includes an independent summation finale (XIV) and an admitted Intermezzo (X). One other variation (XIII) is only tenuously related either to the melody or the structure of the theme. From a technical viewpoint, the Baroque classification of variations as a strict form is comprehensively flouted, whereas Brahms's 'Haydn' Variations and Parry's *Symphonic Variations* are profoundly indebted to the Baroque model. Elgar shared several preoccupations with his contemporaries, including an evident desire to endow the variation form, which ostensibly consists of discrete musical units, with some kind of symphonic coherence. But his angle of approach to this objective was certainly unusual, and some of the reasons for this may reside in the circumstances of conception, and in the musical qualities of the theme itself.

The models Elgar might have followed are already widely divergent, a central division lying with the amount of control exerted by the theme.

Elgar's theme is comparatively long, and it is a fully formed musical utterance, a complete ternary form; more usual is the binary design of the 'Haydn' theme used by Brahms, with repeats, allowing the possibility of varying the repeat itself to make variation within a variation. Brahms's variations are strict, although the theme as melody is scarcely heard again before its apotheosis in the finale. Strictness resides in the derivation of the structure of every variation from the proportions and melodic and harmonic outline of the theme, as if Brahms stripped his source to its essence, using its structure as a template for variations worked out with absolute rigour; their freedom (diversity of texture, colour, tempo, metre) is controlled by close, albeit variable, degrees of adherence to the melody and bass of the theme, and by almost total obedience to its periodic structure, harmonically defined phrases of 5 plus 5 (repeated), then 4 plus 4 plus 7 bars (also repeated). Such strictness underlies the furthest flights of fantasy in the great variation sets of Bach and Beethoven as well as Brahms; these works represent musical abstraction of a high intellectual order, which does not preclude entertainment, even downright fun, as in some of Beethoven's Diabelli variations, the set which perhaps stretches the definition 'strict' to the limit.

Brahms remained one of Elgar's most admired predecessors in the field of symphonic music; and Op. 36, unlike *Froissart*, appears virtually free of the powerful alternative influence, that of Wagner. Yet nothing in the Elgar work sounds like Brahms (whereas a few passages do in his symphonies), and if there is a stylistic influence, it does not lie in his variation technique. In Brahms's Op. 56 the theme-as-tune may be utterly extinguished; nevertheless, there remain regular breaks in the texture when one variation ends and another begins. The architecture consists of regularly disposed blocks in which the component parts are more readily distinguishable than any concept which may govern the whole. Brahms's composition, which scarcely threatens its tonic throughout, poses a question bound to arise in any study of variations: can we hear the work as one piece, or is it better heard as a suite of related pieces? And if we can hear it as one, how can we justify that perception? This question may also be raised with Elgar's *Variations*, and will be considered further in chapter 4.

Dvořák's *Symphonic Variations* is based on a relatively short theme, ternary like Elgar's, and similarly confined to two note-values, crotchet and quaver. On a symphonic pattern one of whose precedents is the finale of Beethoven's *Eroica*, Dvořák extends several of the variations beyond the duration of the theme; he also ventures further from the tonic than Elgar (let alone Brahms), to create a longer set with something of the architecture, as well as the duration, of a long symphonic movement. Dvořák's sharply defined characterisations are surely a precedent, although they signify no comparable 'programme' or portrait-gallery. By contrast to Brahms, Dvořák seems the epitome of freedom, and his frequent changes of tempo and ingenious disguises of the theme might have been Elgar's model. But the overall trajectory is quite different; there are twenty-seven variations (compared to Elgar's thirteen), and the finale begins as an energetic but stylistically retrograde fugue, no more imitated by Elgar than Brahms's passacaglia in Op. 56.

Parry's robust *Symphonic Variations*, in E minor, ending in E major, is based on a short theme of curiously Slavonic cut, yet the generally sober instrumentation more readily suggests Brahms. Parry treats his short original theme with all the respect its author (had he been someone else) could desire. His variations are strict; while they occasionally extend the six-bar pattern of the theme (some simply stretch the material over twelve bars), they never undermine it before the short finale. Parry planned the whole on the lines of a compressed four-movement symphony, but the constant rotations of the theme's underlying pattern and the accumulation of texture at the beginning bring it closer in spirit to Brahms's passacaglia finales (Op. 56, Fourth Symphony) than to his variations. Despite this firm architectural control, Parry keeps his melody, or its principal rhythmic patterns, near the surface, while using related keys for some variations; unity, rather than characterisation, seems to be his aim, and in organisation and aesthetic his variations are remote from Elgar's.

Elgar's variations belong to a genre which might have been called 'caprices on a theme', for which the most distinguished precedents are not orchestral. He links his variations not by underlying phraseology or harmony, but by open adherence to the theme as a melody. Like his predecessors, he climaxes by bringing back the theme, but by this time it has acquired multiple significations from the varied contexts through which it has audibly passed. This method of diversification appears in Schumann's *Etudes symphoniques*, Op. 13 (also known as *Etudes en forme de variations*) and *Carnaval*, piano works which have been mentioned as possible models for Elgar.[5] In *Carnaval* Schumann presents a few pitches represented as letters, and tosses them into a gloriously unstructured set of character-pieces and portraits (including self-portraits as 'Florestan' and 'Eusebius') which, however, he did not call variations. In the *Etudes symphoniques* the variations are strikingly free and strikingly contrasted; they end with an extended finale, and, moreover, some sections are not variations at all (although they are études: in other works Schumann favoured the term 'intermezzo', like Elgar's 'variation' X). Had Op. 13 been given titles like those of *Carnaval* ('Chopin', 'Paganini', 'Chiarina'), the model would be exact.

Elgar's lack of interest in musical parody differentiates his set from Dohnányi's *Variations on a Nursery Song* and comparable exercises in composition *à la manière de* . . . such as the 'Enigma' variations for piano by the leading early nineteenth-century English virtuoso Cipriani Potter, where imitation enlivens essentially ornamental and abstract diversifications of a theme. Another variable in Op. 36 differentiates it from most sets of variations, symphonic or otherwise. Elgar's title and dedication suggest extramusical motivation; and if the nature of his intention remains debatable, its existence, surely, is not. But even this idea is not new; in *Don Quixote*, subtitled 'Fantastic Variations on a Knightly Theme' (1897), Richard Strauss combines the concerto concept with variations as programme music, and his variations are indubitably free, capriccios on a bundle of characteristic motives. Strauss's musical objective is as much contrast as symphonic continuity, at least outside the introduction and finale. Some of Elgar's variations – R.B.T., G.R.S., 'Nimrod', perhaps (***) – are said to have an incident, rather than a personality, as their basis (see chapter 3). Strauss's windmills and sheep and Elgar's bulldog Dan are not, conceptually, so far apart.[6]

The Theme

G minor, *Andante*, 4/4, $\bf{\downarrow} = 63$

The remainder of this chapter will be concerned with the ternary theme to which the improvisation of 21 October 1898 eventually led. In the absence of rigorous structural repetition, the musical qualities of Elgar's variations depend greatly upon the melodic substance of the theme itself (Ex. 2.1). It may be represented formally as A, B, A'. The first part, A (bars 1–6, in G minor, closing on the first beat of bar 7), is the principal material of the whole composition, and it may have been only this part of the theme that Elgar intended by the superscription 'enigma'. The second part, B (bars 7–10, in G major), is subdivided into two distinct motives (B1 and B2, bars 7 and 9). The third section (A') returns to theme A with a strengthened cadence. The sketch of the theme implies an eight-bar B section, bars 5–8 being blank. Theme A is defined by the paired crotchets and quavers which over two bars present a characteristic rhythm and its retrograde.[7] Each bar consists either of two rising and one falling interval, or two falling and one rising (this may seem banal enough until we contrast it with theme B). Given that the most natural melodic movement is by step, the predominance of thirds is striking. Section A curves to a height in the third bar by building up the tonic arpeggio, and returns through the decisive falls of a seventh, as if its strength were failing, to its original pitches.

Motive B1 is characterised by its melodic shape and its dactylic rhythm (crotchet and two quavers), given eight times. Within each one-bar unit the shape is predominantly ascending, the wider interval falling back to its point of departure. The second bar is an exact sequence; the third and fourth bars widen the final interval. Throughout the variations, B1 is strikingly varied in the shapes by which it is represented, but tends to keep its rhythmic character. B2, on the other hand, appears only as a countermelody (flute and oboe, bar 9), inverting the shape of the first four notes in B1. But this falling scale of four (sometimes more) notes is a possible source for a host of passages with varied rhythmic physiognomy. Bars 9–10 are the first taste of thematic counterpoint, which plays such a major role in the variations – unless, indeed, the bass line to theme A, which is mainly scalar, is considered a relative of theme B. B1 throughout is doubled in thirds; thus the predominant melodic interval of theme A is excluded from the melody of B1, but instead is presented vertically.

Section A' restores G minor, its extra bar merely a pause on the final major chord (whereas in bar 7 the last note of section A is elided with section B). A' is much more than a reprise; it replaces the chordal accompaniment, on and off the beat, with an exposed bass-line, and

Ex. 2.1 The theme

Ex. 2.2 Brahms Symphony No. 4 first movement

doubles the theme, initially in sixths. Strict doubling becomes impracticable on reaching the wider intervals of bars 13–14, but the end of bar 12 is already doubled by inversion, prolonged into bar 13. Then, with new inspiration, the middle strings soar up a seventh in a tenor countermelody, which then falls like a variant of B2, all above the bass of section A. The highest pitches of A, B, and A′, the latter two strengthened by Elgar's pointillist instrumentation, occur before their midpoint, so more than half of A′ is declining from a melodic peak (in section A this point is marked pp, bar 4). This could well be an analogue of melancholy or resignation.

Having classified elements of the theme, one might, as with Brahms, devise a thematic template, but reduced to an outline of melody and harmony Elgar's theme does not even fit the first variation.[8] Yet Brahms may have provided a model in aspects of the construction of the theme. In his Fourth Symphony (1885) the passacaglia theme of the finale resembles Elgar's bass, and the main theme of the first movement (Ex. 2.2) is close to Elgar's section A in mood and in its concentration on the interval of a third, mingled with wider intervals.[9] The two ideas share a structural principle of varied repetition. Elgar's section A uses only two metric values, paired crotchets and paired quavers; the second and third units order them the same way as the first. Brahms at first uses only two values, but presents them in a single iambic unit; each phrase is grouped into twice two bars. The two themes both expand their intervals in a second, rhythmically matching, phrase, and each includes a model and its sequence one degree lower. It appears, in this limited comparison, that Elgar is the more inventive; contrary to his reputation as a writer of sequences, he uses them here only on the level of the subphrase (the falling intervals in crotchets form a sequence in each phrase; the quavers go their own ways). But the composers had different objectives; Brahms quickly introduces new rhythmic material, directs his phrase through a local modulation, and drives forward in the manner appropriate to a symphonic exposition. Elgar's continuation (bars 5–6) makes a new play with the two-bar rhythm, shrinking the intervals yet opening the ending by closure on the major third.

I have suggested that Elgar is faithful to his theme as a melody, something which applies not only to its pitches but also to its characteristic rhythm. Ex. 2.3 shows that the physiognomy of A, despite marked local characterisations, is a constant factor which 'goes' over the whole set. Variations VI and VII reduce theme A to a subordinate role (ostinato and accompaniment figure), but all later variations except X and XIII restore its primacy.

The B material is less strictly adhered to, but its influence is felt somewhere in nearly every variation (Ex. 2.4 presents for B the same kind of information as Ex. 2.3). In II, IX, and XIII the derivation from B is too remote to include here (see chapter 3). In VI and VII, B appears more clearly than theme A (there are two versions in VII). The next chapter will relate the transformations of the theme to the character of each variation, and indirectly to the subject of each; the finale is reserved for chapter 4, in which I also discuss ways in which the variation set may be understood as a whole from other points of view than that of the theme which Elgar so resourcefully weaves into his colourful tapestry.

Ex. 2.3 Incipits of theme A showing the rhythmic and melodic departures in each variation

Ex. 2.3 Incipits of theme A showing the rhythmic and melodic departures in each variation

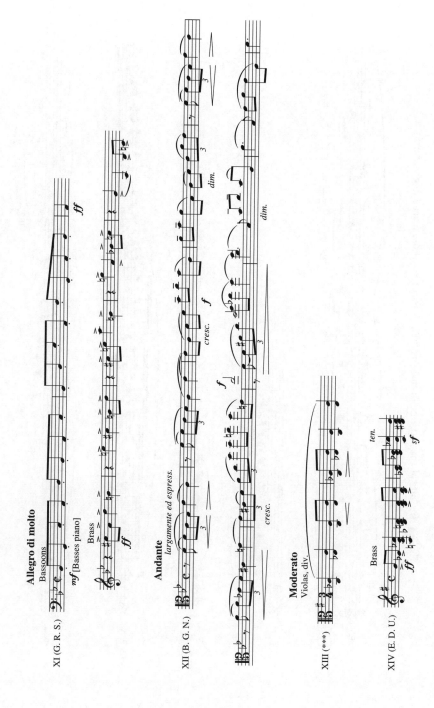

Ex. 2.4 Incipits of the B theme in the variations (other than those placed in chapter 5)

Ex. 2.4 Incipits of the B theme in the variations (other than those placed in chapter 5)

3

Friends pictured within

For an assessment of some variations I draw on Ernest Newman and Donald Tovey, whose remarks gain interest from the fact that they could not identify all the subjects. Comments on the friends not otherwise attributed are drawn from Elgar's own *My Friends Pictured Within* (hereafter *MFPW*), with portraits and the first pages of each variation in a facsimile of the manuscript; the memoirs of Mrs Powell ('Dorabella') and Rosa Burley; and the detective work of Percy M. Young.[1]

Variation I (C.A.E.)

L'istesso tempo (speed of the theme): G minor, *Andante*, 4/4, ♩ = 63

In the MS score Elgar added numbers and initials to each variation. 'I C.A.E.' is placed above the two connecting bars (cue 2), which link the 'personality' of the theme to that of the variation; Elgar himself called C.A.E. 'really a prolongation of the theme' (*MFPW*). There is no comparable lead-in elsewhere in the set, even when variations are in different keys or modes or are played without interruption, and the violins' descent, chromatic and (like B in the theme) lushly doubled in thirds, is not overtly thematic. Ever practical, Elgar uses the time for the second violins to slip on their mutes, which are removed just before the climax (3:4).

There is a second transition within the variation; following the six bars of A, a seventh is added to modulate to E♭ major for B (cue 3). This preliminary refusal of the theme's tonic major contributes much to a characterisation less stable than that of the theme: then, in the third bar, just as we have accepted E♭ as the first clear removal from the tonic, Elgar capriciously switches to G major. Elgar's 'prolongation' reflects the

33

comparatively orthodox formal correspondence to the theme, but the differences profoundly affect expression and structure (see table 3.1).

In its first sketch (folio 2), the variation was closer to the theme. The melody reversed the rhythmic values of the first two bars, and the modulation after six bars is to G major; the rudimentary accompaniment (cello) suggests a piano nocturne. The autograph manuscript still shows many crossings out and changes of detail, 'romantic and delicate additions' to the theme (*MFPW*).

From this music we may infer a personality tender and openly warm but capricious. Moreover, the variation breathes post-Brahmsian passion, not only in the mellow E♭ bars, but in the remarkable seven-layered texture of the A section (table 3.2). The chord-shift from E♭ to D, prepared by the tiniest inflection (A♮, 3:2) and highlighted by texture, moves B2 into the strings as the wind briefly rest (3:3). The return to A′ is broached by an interrupted cadence in G *minor* (D7 to E♭, 3:5) at the top of a crescendo; A is given to brass, the first trumpet entry and the first *fortissimo*, the reprise of A in its original rhythmic values (as in the theme) being overlaid by a development of B2, a magnificent two-octave descent. Into this moment one might read any kind of climax: Newman called it 'noble'.

Other features contribute to a symbolic interpretation. When the opening texture is restored (4:3), the melody is raised two octaves in mid-phrase from horns and cellos to flute. The harmony is softened (not the diminished seventh of the theme, 1:5, but an augmented sixth); the theme's plagal cadence is evaded (the D bass is prolonged for two bars to reach a perfect cadence); and the two final tonic bars are decorated by the first major-mode statement of theme A (clarinet). Elgar's term 'prolongation' may refer to this cadence, where the theme is at last harmonically resolved, signifying the wholeness of marriage ('Mann und Weib, und Weib und Mann reichet an die Gottheit an').[2]

Tovey described the variation as a 'glorification' of the theme. Powell includes it among variations which constitute a 'portrait', and identified the 'whistle', Elgar's call to C.A.E. on arriving home. This variation, which Kennedy calls 'radiant and serene', may be read as a tribute to C.A.E., who is summoned (whistle motive), shows caprice and a passion not normally imputed to Alice, and is idealised in the coda: soulmate, poet, helpmeet, a lady Reed called 'sweet, loveable'.[3]

Table 3.1. *Differences between the theme and the first variation*

	Theme	Var. I: (C.A.E.)
Design	A–B–A′	lead-in–A–B–A′–[coda B]
Phrasing A–B–A′	6–4–7	[2]–7–4–6 [coda 4]
Texture of A	Simple: two elements	Complex: seven elements
Texture of B	Simple: B2 counterpoint in third bar	Counterpoint B2 in every bar
Texture of A′	New counterpoint, bar 13	B2 developed in counterpoint to A
Tonality A–B–A′	g–G–g	[G–g in the link] g–E♭–G–g–G
Bass of theme B	G then D; sustained	E♭ then D; intermittent attack
Orchestra A–B–A′	A strings	A full except trumpets, percussion
	B plus woodwind	B as theme
	A′ reduced	A′ tutti, reduced in coda
Dynamics	All quiet	Flux *pp[p]* – *ff* – *ppp*

Table 3.2. *The texture of Variation I (C.A.E.)*

Layer	Instruments	Material
1	1st flute, 1st clarinet, 2nd violins, violas	Theme
2	Oboe, bassoon	Whistle
3	2nd flute, 2nd clarinet	Interlocking counterpoint using values of layers 1 and 2
4	1st violins, 1st cellos	Syncopated arpeggios
5	2nd cellos, pizz., second note of each group sustained by 4th horn	Nocturne accompaniment
6	Double basses (timpani for one note), 1st, 2nd, 3rd horns	Bass line from theme; off-beat chords
7	Trombones, timpani	Chorale (bar 7), roll

35

The female is seen here through the male gaze, of course, but how could it be otherwise?

Variation II (H.D.S-P.)

G minor, *Allegro*, 3/8, $\downarrow$. = 72

The design is ternary (introduction, middle, coda), but the middle is theme A and theme B is sidelined. The character of the variation lies in the 'quaint semiquaver figure' (Newman), exposed on its own over the first seventeen bars; when partly doubled by legato woodwind (from 5:8, see Ex. 3.1), its contour resembles theme B, and its falling second bar recalls the counterpoint at bar 14 of the theme. The music begins mock-fugally: mock, because the second entry (bar 3, on the dominant) is unaccompanied and the third, on the subdominant, returns to the first violins rather than bringing in a new voice. Slippery wind lines are superimposed and bars 5:10–13 are a sequence of 5:6–9 up a fifth. The dynamic reaches *forte*, and a four-bar diminuendo is completed at the entry of theme A (6:1).

Theme A enters like a *cantus firmus*, exaggerating the rhythmic values of the theme (see Ex. 2.3). Elgar could no doubt have composed the opening motive to fit the theme like a contrapuntal glove, but the first seventeen bars do not do this; instead the string figure is developed, incorporating scale-fragments, and is recoloured, on high woodwind. Theme A is itself developed, interpolating a sequence of sevenths (from 6:9). With a sustained viola line of leaping fourths, three-note figures in second violins and woodwind, and clarinet arpeggios, there are five textural strands from 6:7, yet the music remains transparent. Theme A resumes its normal course (6:13) and growls to a halt as the texture reduces (but note the delicate pizzicato doubling the semiquavers). The rest (cue 7) is coda, the semiquaver figure playfully passed around, mainly on tonic and dominant pitches, handed back to the wind, and fragmented by rests. Note the rhythm of A touched in as a timpani solo, and the weird ascending counterpoint of tritone, fourth, tritone, major third, and tritone. This, like the ladder of (mainly) fourths in the last movement of Berlioz's *Symphonie fantastique* (bar 11), would do credit to an atonal composer (7:5).

The opening suggests a busy search; after the contrapuntal develop-

Ex. 3.1 Derivation of H.D.S-P. from theme B

ment against a grumbling theme A, the sparse coda, its plagal cadence touched in pizzicato, suggests it was unsuccessful. No *tierce de Picardie* is even implied; this is the first section to *end* in G minor. Correspondence between this waspish miniature and the amiable Steuart-Powell resides only in his competent piano playing; not he, but a habit, his 'characteristic diatonic run over the keys before beginning to play, is here humorously travestied' in semiquaver figures 'chromatic beyond H.D.S-P.'s liking' (*MFPW*).

Variation III (R.B.T.)

G major, *Allegretto*, 3/8, ♪=144

The form reflects the theme's ABA' but (uniquely) repeats B-A' to produce ABA'BA'. Elgar transforms the contour of A into a waltz-like scherzo; this involves repeating some notes while omitting others, and reversing the pitches of bar 3 (see Ex. 2.3). Tempo and key-signature recall II; but, since two quaver beats equal the previous whole bar, III is slower (it can be three times the length of II in performance). The texture, at first wind-dominated, has two strands: the tune Elgar called 'pert' (oboe, thirds and sevenths picked out by flute and pizzicato violins) and accompanying parallel sixths (clarinets, flute, and bassoon). There is no bass until the C♯ of bar 8 (corresponding to bar 6 of the theme).

Variation III is the first in G major, its brightness enhanced by the D♯ in bar 2 under the first notes of the theme. The sharp side is developed further when the B–A' section takes a nose-dive into F♯ major. B1 is chromatically compressed (clarinets), and the falling fourth is handed to violins. At this tempo a four-bar B section would have seemed perfunctory: 9:5 begins as a rescored repeat of 9:1, but develops against a bass counterpoint; the rhythm persists repetitively in the violins' version of B2. The cadence in the local dominant, C♯, is on the surface a conventional move little exploited in *Variations* (until the finale).[4] At cue 10 a return to A would be timely, but the tonality is astray by a tritone. The sequential bass figure (unlike the coda figure of II) sequentially ornaments triads of D and E♭: essentially the passage circles the dominant, D. These bars, which form a retransition, include fragments of both themes in the rhythms particular to this variation. A' is essentially A repeated, counterpointed by what Elgar called the bassoon's 'growing grumpiness'.

Newman found this 'whimsical'; Tovey identified 'a kind of Mazurka'. Elgar recalled that Richard Baxter Townshend, related by marriage to W.M.B. and often a guest at Hasfield, once impersonated 'an old man in amateur theatricals – the low voice flying off occasionally into "soprano" timbre' (Burley suggests his voice had never quite broken). It follows that the variation does not picture Townshend as his normal self, and Powell includes it among the 'caricatures'. At most, however, Elgar's memory applies to the retransition; it has no connection with the engaging oboe tune, nor with the delicate modulation to F♯ for the B section. Indeed, heard without preconception, it might well depict the young Ivor Atkins (see chapter 1); while enjoying its skittish charm, we can legitimately forget Townshend the traveller, author, scholar, eccentric, and tricyclist whom Young considers 'in many ways the most dynamic and original' of the subjects.[5]

Variation IV (W.M.B.)

G minor, *Allegro di molto*, 3/4, ♩.=572

Variation IV, with thirty-two one-beat bars, is the shortest, occupying less than half a minute. There is continuity, however, in the metronome marking; the bar-length is that of II. IV is among the closest in design, if not in spirit, to the theme, restoring the alternate quavers and crotchets (but removing the rests), and retaining most of the same pitches; A takes six bars and B expands over eight.[6] However, ten bars are added from cue 13 to form an interlude. After the spareness and low dynamic level of II and III this rumbustious opening has irresistible force. For A' (cue 14), Elgar knew better than merely to amplify A by replacing *ff* with *fff* (although he does this). The string texture, compressed in A, expands in both directions; the bass line is reinforced, and the three notes available to the timpani are used throughout, whereas in A eight beats lacked percussion. Oboes and clarinets go up an octave, strengthened by flutes (rested in A); trombones are added; and the low pumping of trumpets becomes a vigorous thematic contribution.

In B surging sequences are counterpointed to diatonic scales in the strings, and the squareness of the passage is emphasised by regular timpani rolls. The last bar before cue 13 suddenly accents the second beat (as, implicitly, does the first bar of the variation). This gives rise to the interlude, in which the oboes play A in full, at the original pitch; the clarinets follow in strict canon one crotchet behind and a fifth lower, causing maximum rhythmic and tonal disruption. Elgar's pointed sevenths are reinforced by the strings, and 13:1–6 seem about to be repeated a fifth higher at 13:7. But the dominant here is major, and timpani, horn, and basses restore order with a dominant pedal, crescendo.

Newman called it 'breezy and boisterous', but Tovey heard a 'frightful temper'; yet Burley calls the subject 'bluff and genial'. Powell, who knew him as a relation, includes this among the 'caricatures'. Hasfield Court was a manor bought with 'new money' and inherited by the hospitable sportsman and lover of music, William Meath Baker, more the friend of Alice than of Elgar.[7] It appears that Baker '*forcibly* read out the arrangements for the day and hurriedly left the music-room, with an inadvertent bang of the door'; for Elgar the canonic middle section suggested 'the teasing attitude of the guests'.

Variation V (R.P.A.)

C minor, *Moderato,* ♩ = 63

Contrary to the usual trend, Elgar increased the speed from ♩ = 58 in the sketch, to restore the tempo of the theme, but variation V matches the rondo-like scheme of III, here without recourse to a repeat

Ex. 3.2 Derivation of R.P.A. from theme B

15

(ABA'B'A''). The variation is fully cadenced onto 18:4, but the music continues in motion on a tonic pedal, so that its last note is also the first note of VI; the C major of VI also provides V with its *tierce de Picardie*.

Rhythmically, V is complicated by a principal theme in 12/8 counterpointed to theme A in its original 4/4 (Ex. 3.2). The combination requires the second bar of A to be one step lower than normal, yet for three beats there would be no difficulty with the original version. Elgar must have realised this, and he could have rewritten the last beat to fit. Instead he preferred the palindromic rhythm of theme A to be matched to its pitches, while the new melody retains the obsessiveness inherent in its returns to C. The tune matches the sequential sevenths with its own sequence (bars 3–4), and rolls back to the dominant, the violins' sonorous open G.

This variation may have been sketched late. Its characterising new melody may be related to B2.[8] Perhaps for this reason, B1 is rapidly dismissed, forming only the connecting semiquaver flute figure in 16:1 (see Ex. 2.4); this is elegantly inverted by the clarinet in 16:4, leading to the reprise of A. The B section has its own principal idea (16:2–3) designed for maximum contrast: staccato, light in articulation, something like a waltz, and emphasised by horn harmony in a homophonic texture (its stepwise descent might be related to B2). The dance quality is enhanced by the pizzicato arpeggios (16:3), where the violins join the melody. This charming confection is firmly suppressed by the ripely reorchestrated A'. The texture is inverted, strings below wind, and trumpets support the sevenths. The melody is sequentially extended, and the theme itself develops a descending sequence (17:5–7) to fall as far as F, which is the first bass note of 16:2; Elgar takes the opportunity to cut the original B1 bar (16:1), reducing the B′ section to three bars. Section A″ is a coda, weighted by timpani rolls, internal melodic repetition (four-fold falling sevenths), and elimination of all but the first four notes of the melody. The coda is darkly coloured by the hitherto silent trombones; the main rhythm throbbing on the bottom note of the cellos adds a note of menace.

Newman noted the contrast between 'gravity' (the A section; Tovey suggests 'gloomy') and 'cheery chatter', a musical design which makes its point without specific reference to the grandson of Arnold of Rugby. For Powell this variation, her favourite, was a 'portrait' of Richard Arnold, a pleasant man who seems to have wasted his talents (Young). He played the piano 'in a self-taught manner, evading difficulties but suggesting in a mysterious way the real feeling' (*MFPW*; did Elgar remember *The Importance of Being Earnest?*). His 'serious conversation was continually broken up by whimsical and witty remarks' (section B, in which Powell heard his characteristic laugh).

Variation VI (Ysobel)

C major, *Andantino* 3/2, ♩=48

The sketch suggests this delicious vignette was conceived at a slower tempo (♩=69); the overall form is like V (ABAB and coda on A). Like II and V, VI has its own motive in counterpoint to the theme. The 'Ysobel' motive occurs in every bar, theme A (or its first three notes, doubled in thirds) being reduced to accompaniment. Various instruments intervene to stabilise the otherwise attenuated texture. At cue 20, after only five bars, the bassoon thirds extend B1 over a tenth, forming a morphological connection with the 'Ysobel' motive (see Ex. 2.4). The four-bar B section ends when this motive is freely inverted (again bassoons, 20:4), leading to a much-varied repetition of the whole nine-bar unit from cue 21. The A section now has a poignant solo viola countermelody, and the 'Ysobel' motive is delicately pointed by clarinet arpeggios. The B material (cue 22) is more strongly orchestrated and the violins pick up the motive in a brief surge of passion, not unlike the similar moment in C.A.E. The link in 22:4, a new sequential descent of B1 over a chromatic bass, adds playful interjections of 'Ysobel' in the wind. The four-bar coda, based on the A section, ends with the solo viola having the last word.

Isabel Fitton, a violin student of Elgar (Young), was tall (this is allegedly encoded in the 'Ysobel' motive) and part of a large family of musically active amateurs. She helped correct proofs of *Caractacus* with the Norbury sisters in the summer of 1898. She was an 'amateur viola player' (*MFPW*); her motive represents 'a difficulty for beginners' (crossing from the open C string to e' on the D string; the bow must avoid the intervening G string). Newman found VI 'very serious, sombre, and contemplative'. One might query his first two epithets; Elgar called it 'pensive' but 'for a moment, romantic'. Powell considers VI, with II and XII, to be inspired by the instrument more than the person; but understanding this early viola joke should not be allowed to detract from the delicate counterpoint and meditative beauty of the whole.

Variation VII (Troyte)

C major, *Presto*, 1/1, ○=76

The unusual time-signature requires one beat in a bar. The overt contrast with 'Ysobel' disguises similarities in form. A is again subordinated, now into a tonic and dominant ostinato, set up by timpani and maintained by the low strings; but it is fiercely independent, asserting a 3/4 rhythm (Ex. 2.3).[9] The melodic part of the A section is actually B1, with two upward surges and a long fall (see Ex. 2.4: note the rhythmic palindrome in the fall, however, which corresponds to a feature of theme A). In section A this twelve-bar unit is repeated with fuller scoring (and an attempt by the woodwind to complete the shape of theme B1 at 24:6). The descent skids through a chromatic A♭ (24:12) to gain half a bar. Contrast in the shorter (ten-bar) B section (cue 25) is textural: the ostinato stops, roaring trombones play B1 in C minor, and wild violins establish a near-ostinato in the treble. An augmented sixth chord arrives midway in 25:9, the misplaced accent creating metric uncertainty, and the wind, sensationally, run with it (the trumpet is the bass) to land forcefully on C minor. However, this bar brings back the ostinato and the A section (now 12 plus 8 bars), the violins emphasising C major in scales of improbable velocity. After the second B section a seven-bar coda allows us to hear A in the full glory of brass, but rudely truncated before the descending sevenths. The violence is exuberant, not threatening. Tovey heard Shaw's Henry Higgins; Newman calls the C minor section 'a raging, tearing propaganda', and the 'exceedingly impetuous' whole 'as invigorating as a walk over the mountains with sun and wind'.[10] But it is hardly the kind of talkative walk around Malvern on which Arthur Troyte Griffith did indeed accompany Elgar. Professionally an architect, artist, and stage designer, 'Troyte' probably met the Elgars in 1896 or 1897 and was a lifelong friend; he helped the Elgars deal with house-agents. For his height Elgar called him 'Ninepin' (Powell, p. 13). Powell considers VII a 'caricature'; Elgar referred to 'some maladroit essays to play the pianoforte' (theme A is reduced to a two-finger exercise). Griffith was the long-standing secretary of the Malvern Concert Club. Descriptions of his social manner vary between very quiet and curt in speech; he was a determined adversary in an argument who took on G. B. Shaw (Young).

Variation VIII (W.N.)

G major, *Allegretto*, 6/8, $\; \downarrow \! . = 52$ [$\downarrow = 104$]

The sketch suggests $\downarrow \! . = 58$ ($\downarrow = 174$), so Elgar had already reduced the tempo before noting (on Richter's suggestion) 'a leetle slower'.[11] This variation restores the ternary design of the theme while remaining throughout in the major. The upward extensions of the opening pattern of A ally this with the normally contrasting B1, since they are now both based on the rising tetrachord B–C–D–E (see Exx. 2.3 and 2.4). Nevertheless, a marked contrast remains. A consists of upward surges (wind) and a fall (strings) based on the descending thirds; the lines are doubled in sixths, more open than the thirds predominant elsewhere. The music is purely diatonic for four bars; bars 5–8, identical in orchestral layout, appear to repeat but are subtly inflected, by chromatic touches and inverting the order of the rhythmic units into a different dynamic pattern (compare 30:3, 30:7). B1 chuckles for two bars, but its descending phase (from 31:3, modelled on B2) is laden with sighs and counterpointed to A. The next four bars begin with a marvellous cello solo, with 31:7 a step higher than its model (31:3). 31:9–10 are an added climax before the reprise of A: this marks the first two bars by the piccolo, and 32:5–6 by trills from the B section.

As a compositional miniature, this would be hard to surpass. Newman heard it as 'feminine', its rhythm 'of engaging lightness'; but W.N. was athletic as well as musical (Young). The sketches bear the note 'secys', suggesting an intention to honour Winifred Norbury and Monica Hyde, secretaries to the Worcestershire Philharmonic Society. Winifred helped correct proofs of *Caractacus* with Isabel Fitton in summer 1898, as did her sister Florence who, according to their niece, was more frivolous; with Dora Penny, Florence's role 'was to get him ready for work' whereas Winifred and Lady Mary Lygon 'could keep him in order and *make* him work as well as amuse him'.[12] Winifred 'was more connected with music than others of the family; to justify this position a little suggestion of a characteristic laugh is given' (*MFPW*). The obvious candidate for this is the B section (cue 31: Burley specifies the falling woodwind figure), but her niece said her laugh was like 'a deep bell' to which nothing in the variation corresponds unless it is the background support provided by the horns at cue 31. The trills suggested to Powell her laugh or 'the triangle that she played in the Philharmonic orchestra', but the triangle is not used. In any case, Elgar tells us that the persona of the variation is really the eighteenth-century Norbury house, Sherridge, near Malvern, epitome of an ideal civilisation in a rural environment.

Variation IX (Nimrod)

E♭ major, *Adagio*, 3/4, ♩=52

Nearly all commentators praise not only the nobility of this variation (Elgar used the direction *nobilmente*, but only in the piano version), but its simplicity. It is close to the theme in melody, form, and disposition of the main motives of theme A, although the opening takes on a distinguishing pattern with a fall of the fourth in the second bar (f′ replacing the expected g′). The quaver pairs are on first and third beats, the falling sevenths on second and first beats, yet the phrasing is intricate; note the difference between bar 1, completing the link from VIII, and bar 9. Sonorous beauty results from flexible division of strings, and counterpoint: the bass plays three notes of the theme in retrograde (C,

Ex. 3.3 'Nimrod', showing derivation of the B section from the theme

G, B♭), then the middle voice (33:3–4) typically resolves a leading note (A♮) down to the dominant. Although immediately neutralised by A♭, this A♮ returns when the sevenths make a large but irregular sequence (this touchstone of character is, however, anticipated in II).[13] A dominant cadence is narrowly evaded, the bass descending in fifths to the tonic at cue 34. This reprise of the A section is expanded over eleven bars, diverging into another irregular sequence and conquering a higher register; the descent is mirrored by an aspiring middle voice (cellos) resembling the counterpoint in the A′ section of the theme (34:8–11). The scoring is enriched but not yet full, and the perfect cadence is evaded: Elgar has his eye on the enhanced version of these bars from cue 36.

This is delayed by the B section (eight bars, from cue 35), essentially a dominant prolongation and thus far removed from the context of B in the theme. Its connection to the theme has been doubted, but the cello plays an eloquent synthesis of 'B' elements, B2 with the rhythmic proportions of B1 (Ex. 3.3); the falling woodwind intervals (as in 35:4) could also originate in B1. Too often vulgarised, the climax is coloured with tender care: note the rests in the brass parts, the sequence handed down to soaring cellos and violas (36:5), and the reticence of the flutes. A halt is called when an A♭ replaces the expected G (compare 34:10 with 36:9) and the next bar, a rhetorical *largamente* on an A♭ minor chord, could foretell a yet grander climax. But the four-bar coda is a swift deflation, the diminuendo by orchestral elimination as well as surface dynamics. There is no sense of incompleteness, but enough is withheld to justify the recurrence of part of this variation during the finale.

A. J. Jaeger came from Düsseldorf, a fact of some importance for

Elgar's reputation there. He became one of Novello's editors, and besides contributing to the house magazine, *The Musical Times*, he published notes on Elgar's music. Newman, who recognised the dedicatee, called 'Nimrod' 'grave and composed'; 'its final statement is extremely dignified, glowing with the richest of colour, and breathing some of the most elevated inspiration that modern music can show'. Powell insists that the variation is *not* a portrait of the man she describes as voluble and with an 'amusing – almost racy – turn of phrase'; Burley emphasised the incongruity of music and subject (but she called Jaeger 'a commonplace German' and deplored his musical influence). Elgar said that 'something ardent and mercurial' was needed to complete the portrait. He had already confided to Jaeger: 'I have omitted your outside manner & have only seen the good loveable honest SOUL in the middle of you! and the music's not good enough . . .'[14]

'Nimrod' is founded on the gratitude Elgar felt for his principal London supporter and adviser, but its mood may have been determined by an incident. According to Powell, Jaeger talked him out of a depression, partly by citing Beethoven's example. Elgar only reported that the variation was 'the record of a long summer evening talk, when my friend discoursed eloquently on the slow movements of Beethoven . . . it will be noticed that the opening bars are made to suggest the slow movement of the Eighth Sonata (Pathétique)'.[15] But for Elgar's comment, this resemblance might have escaped notice, particularly as it is unaffected by the melodic alteration to the second bar specific to this variation (see appendix); the theme is in any case closer to the opening of the A♭ sonata Op. 110.

Through irreversible processes of association, 'Nimrod' has acquired an independent life as a national elegy (yet XII is more elegiac in mood). 'Nimrod' is now as much part of the musical representation of England (sometimes Britain) as the trio of the first *Pomp and Circumstance* March and the tune in Holst's *Jupiter*. Elgar was the first to slow 'Nimrod' from its original Moderato ($\downharpoonleft$ =66 in the autograph score); on his 1926 recording it begins more like $\downharpoonleft$ =40–44, and some modern performances are even slower (see chapter 6). Elgar encouraged the elegiac connection by quoting this form of the theme in *The Music Makers* (cue 51) at 'But one man's soul it hath broken'. By then Jaeger was dead. But the variation was not composed as an elegy and its regular appearance, in a medium adapted to any function – it has been transcribed for piano solo, for organ, and for recorder quintet, as well as military or brass bands – is based on a misunderstanding of its inspiration. Unfortunately, it appeals not only to sentiments of resignation but to patriotism and even xenophobia.[16] In 1997, 'Nimrod' was heard at the last sunset of the British Empire (the handing over of Hong Kong) and at the funeral of Diana, Princess of Wales.

X (Dorabella) (Intermezzo)

G major, *Allegretto*, 3/4, ♩=80

The intermezzo is justly loved and like 'Nimrod' was published separately. From a possible early origin it could have migrated to *The Wand of Youth* had it not come to hand in 1898. It falls into a subtle, though seemingly simple, design defined by double bars, and has unusually wide tonal reference for Op. 36; the thematic material (string flickers and woodwind punctuation) is readily adaptable to any harmonic situation.

In section A (38 bars) the main phrase goes to B minor (38:9), and is then developed against a ghostly solo viola to reach the very remote F♯ minor (39:10–40:1). From cue 40 the woodwind figure is replaced by a chromatic inversion of its general shape. Elgar moves to an ambiguous harmony (half-diminished seventh on G, to cue 41) and slips neatly into a reprise (41–2), cadencing in G. In section B (42:2–44:1) the violas lead each three-bar phrase with a sweeping scale of concentrated energy. The internal contrast of texture is marked: strings dominate, legato – the octave doubling of the inner part (second violins, violas) is characteristic – and wind colour the cadences. No less marked is the change of tonal orientation, conveying G minor but with cadences on B♭, D minor, and again B♭. The last wriggles by a chain of fifths to the augmented sixth chord (43:5) used in the theme (bar 5); again, Elgar slips sideways into G major. The remainder restates the reprise of A (44–5 follow 41–2). A reprise of B (cue 45) remains in G major despite an attractive sliding sequence in clarinet and bassoons; four bars of A, in which the strings adhere firmly to G major chords, round it off.

'Dorabella' is no variation, although A is detectable at the opening

(Ex. 2.3), and the viola countermelody (formally within the A section) outlines the opening of B (Ex. 2.4). Here and in XIII we recall Elgar's warning that 'the connexion between the Variations and the Theme is often of the slightest texture' (see p. 65). Newman saw no link with the theme, finding 'a dainty, sinuous melody of the most winsome charm'; as with 'Ysobel', he could not miss the sex of the subject. Dora Penny, daughter of a widowed clergyman who later married the sister of W.M.B., was an intimate of Hasfield and of the Elgar household; Elgar nicknamed her 'Dorabella' from 'Mozart's *Così fan tutti*' (*sic* in *MFPW*). She overheard him in creative moods, and was soon privy to *Variations*. She also danced to his music, including her own intermezzo, and was a frequent companion on bicycle rides. Her music, not as overtly pastoral as W.N., evokes the peaceful companionship which she describes (*Memories, passim*; see also Young). She recognised her minor speech defect in the woodwind figure, a little stutter marked by the tenuto on the first semiquaver, sometimes exaggerated in performances (including, oddly, Toscanini's). Elgar never teased her other than through this pretty detail, which could be sung to her nickname 'Dorabella'. Sad to say, the Elgars eventually 'dropped' her (and Rosa Burley) from their circle of friends. In *MFPW* he says only, and drily, that the 'inner sustained phrases at first on the viola and later on the flute should be noted'.

Variation XI (G.R.S.)

G minor, *Allegro di molto*, 2/2, $\downarrow$=100

XI erupts with a plummeting string figuration, carefully interlocked (sections enter successively a third above the end of the previous one). Bars 2–3 reduce the first sixteen notes of A to rapid quavers in the double basses and bassoons; bars 4–5 complete an imperfect cadence with B1. Elgar has thus compressed most of the seventeen-bar theme into six seconds. Not surprisingly, he begins the process again, quietly, but the bass A of bar 4 now (cue 48) supports B1 a fifth higher; A major, two dominant removes from the tonic, forms a brilliant platform for the brass to declaim theme A with its original values. This three-phrase unit constitutes a bold exposition (section A); from cue 49 a ten-bar development drives the bass by steps from A down to D ready for a reprise. The rhythmic units of the theme are reduced to a military tattoo in the bass; at 49:3 a double fugato begins, one subject being A (as it appeared in 47:2–3), the other the opening flurry: of course they combine to perfection. There are four entries, every two bars, in G minor, D minor, a sort of E♭ major spiced by F♯s, and again G minor. The recapitulation gives out the brassy A on a D major chord, at 50:5. That could have been it (perhaps with a *tierce de Picardie*). But in perhaps the most musically inventive of all the set, Elgar presents the version of A peculiar to this variation in counterpoint to the sequence of sevenths – a second double fugato – and holds G minor for the last four bars, thematically another combination of theme B1 with the string flourish.

George Robertson Sinclair, the only professional musician among the friends, moved in 1889 from Truro to Hereford as cathedral organist. Newman recognised the initials, but commented only on 'sudden breaks and wild rushes . . . an abruptly explosive kind of energy'. According to Powell, Sinclair sat 'very stiff and straight' at Mrs Hyde's tea-party, and one passage (perhaps the second fugato) recalled to an acquaintance his stiff and brisk walk. Powell reports the theory that theme A in bars 2–3 was inspired by Sinclair's superb organ-pedalling, and the dense contrapuntal elements are a show of compositional virtuosity in strict style, with its church-music associations. Elgar, however, denied any connection 'with organs and cathedrals', and located the germ of the variation in an adventure of bulldog Dan; unless Dan wore a bell collar, however, only bicycling explains the prominence of the triangle, and the sheer speed and energy of the variation reflect Sinclair's cycling, which left Elgar well behind.[17] Various accounts (e.g. Young) agree that Sinclair threw his stick, Dan plunged into the Wye (bar 1), paddled vigorously after it (bars 2–3), and emerged with a self-satisfied bark (bar 5, distantly related to B1, is marked 'Dan' in the sketch, folio 12v). But Elgar says that Dan fell down the steep bank. 'G.R.S. said, "Set that to music". I did; here it is.'[18] Elgar habitually jotted down ideas, which he called 'the moods of Dan', in Sinclair's visitors' book; these notations were often recycled, with some lack of decorum, for instance as the prayer in *Gerontius*.[19] Reed sensibly pointed out that the organist and dog-owning interpretations are compatible; both conform to the musical facts.[20]

Variation XII (B.G.N.)

G minor, *Andante*, 4/4, $\downarrow$=58

This variation was certainly conceived early (see chapter 1), and is closer to the theme than most, constituting a reprise before the departures of XIII and the finale. It is the only variation to make more than passing use of the most conventional of techniques for ornamenting a theme, filling its intervals of a third with passing- and neighbour-notes (see Ex. 2.3). It also adheres to the ternary form of the theme, but not to its exact proportions: after a two-bar introduction, A has ten bars, B six, A' eight, and the introduction is repeated as a coda. This is the cello variation; the frame (like the 'Ysobel' coda) is a solo, closely based on A, and arching to the tenor register of the instrument which is exploited by unison cellos in the variation proper. Violas are added from 52:7; in 52:9, perhaps to avoid a technical difficulty, the cellos hold d'' rather than falling a seventh. An oboe is added to cover this moment; the gentle violin echo (53:1) holds d''' as if in sympathy.

The extension of the A section, after four bars close to the theme, is achieved by a large-scale harmonic sequence – common enough for nineteenth-century music but rarer in the miniatures which constitute *Variations*. Bar 7 begins the theme all over again a third higher, but Elgar's sequences are not mechanically exact: where the first phrase remained close to G minor, this moves from B♭ to D minor (52:8). Cue 53 brings D major harmony as the aspiring sequence falls back, but only to B♭ (53:4). Here the B section begins, in which two tunes are equally weighted: a continually varied palette of wind instruments part-doubled by second violins (theme B1) and the viola–cello group ruminating on the patterns of the A section (see Ex. 2.4). Cue 54 begins a compressed A', rising to a swiftly defused climax (compare C.A.E.) and preserving the move to B♭ (54:5), so that the coda is needed to return home; even here, however, resolution in G minor is cheated by the opening of XIII. Elgar ended the sketch on G and provided a single bar of G *minor* for separate performance of XII, but in normal performance the curious result is a viola slur extended into the void.

Newman noted the 'dignified climax, and a finely spiritual effect' at the end. Powell included B.G.N. among variations inspired by the instrument; perhaps it reflects more the soul of the cello, an instrument beloved of Elgar, than of Basil Nevinson, a fellow Conservative whose 'very dear' friendship may have been helped by an absence of professional involvement (unlike his brother, a solicitor, and his cousin, an architect). He himself was a non-practising barrister 'whose scientific and artistic attainments, and the whole-hearted way they were put at the disposal of his friends, particularly endeared him to the writer' (*MFPW*).[21]

XIII (***) (Romanza)

G major, *Moderato*, 3/4, ♩=76

A ternary design with a coda based on the B section is simple enough; but this variation is characterised by frustration. Its ten-bar A section follows the pattern of some earlier variations ('Nimrod', G.R.S.) in its early return to the opening (55:6; the cadence with échappé echoes 'Ysobel', 19:4–5). But instead of renewing this idea and letting it blossom, as is normal in *Variations*, the wind repeat the opening descent more slowly (see Ex. 3.4), regularising the initially syncopated pattern and falling off without returning to the more expansive music of bars 3–5. Instead, the harmony moves via C to A♭ (comparable to the G–E♭ move from W.N. to 'Nimrod').[22] At cue 59 (A') these ten bars meet a similar fate, using E♭, the submediant of G minor, not G major.

After so much ingenious integration of A and B sections ('Nimrod',

Ex. 3.4 XIII, the opening

G.R.S., B.G.N.), they are here disconnected in every way. Lilting grace is spiritually crushed by the very quiet, obstinate repetitions, a B section unmistakably driving home the rhythm of A. Apart from a confirmatory cadence (to cue 57), this viola ostinato endures for sixteen bars, backed by a barely audible solo cello C; side-drum sticks do nothing to clarify the pitch of the timpani (nominally C).[23] Above this the clarinet twice intones 'a phrase from Mendelssohn's "Calm Sea and Prosperous Voyage"' (*MFPW*) – the three-note motive is in quotation marks – at a far slower tempo than the original, and with an elegantly curving extension. The clarinet leads the harmony to F minor where the noise element ('the distant throb of the engines of a liner') is moved to the bass drum and a vast musical space is covered by the ostinato; the trombones (not in quotes) intone Mendelssohn's motive in the minor mode. A sixth (d) added to F minor adroitly restores G major, but lyricism is still not allowed its head in the A' section. In the coda the ostinato, transposed down a fourth, is turned by the ending of the clarinet phrase back to a G chord, which is major, but only just.

Newman noted, as with 'Dorabella', that there is hardly any reference to the theme, so that the Romanza is another intermezzo; Tovey calls it 'a free episode . . . the most romantic thing in the work', but Shera detected theme B in the opening phrases (he does not explain how).[24] This pattern of falling fourths a third apart occurs in at least two earlier works, an E major epiphany in the *Serenade* for strings (finale, bar 60) and the G major organ sonata, composed as recently as 1895.[25] In preparing the piano arrangement, Elgar hesitated, eliminating the Mendelssohn reference by changing the clarinet's c'' to a' (with equivalent adjustments later): the melody would thus match the opening of the variation, in elongated rhythm.[26]

Musical shapes, however, are the lesser enigma attached to this variation than the question: who is (***)? When proposing to eliminate the Mendelssohn quotation, Elgar commented: 'The pretty Lady is on the sea & far away & I meant this (originally) as a little quotation from Mendelssohn's Meerestille u. Glückliche Fahrt. – but I did not acknowledge it as the critics – if one mentions anything of the kind – talk of nothing else.'[27] Later he wrote that 'the asterisks take the place of the name of a lady who was, at the time of the composition, on a sea voyage' (*MFPW*). Memory played him false; Lady Mary Lygon visited the

Elgars on the day the full score was finished, and only sailed to Australia in April 1899, accompanying her brother, Lord Beauchamp, who was to become governor of New South Wales. The story, however, was propagated by Dora Powell and Ivor Atkins (who were on the scene), and is repeated even today.[28] As a dynamic element in the musical life of the region, choral conductor, educator, and organiser of a festival at Madresfield Court, Lady Mary Lygon was surely worth a portrait, and XIII ('L.') is marked as 'finished' in the early catalogue of variations (Burley says she heard it before the end of 1898).[29] So why the seascape? In 1906, Newman, already propagating the story that the subject was on a voyage at the time of composition, remarked that 'the marine picture becomes still more lovely' at the climax. Fifty years later, having in the meantime become acquainted, from Elgar himself, with the weight of emotion attached to it, he read it quite differently, hearing 'pregnant brooding upon some personal experience . . . throbbing engines . . . dwelling in imagination on somebody or something the parting from whom and which had at some time or other torn the very heart out of him'.[30] I shall return to this point in chapter 5.

4

A form of self-portraiture

XIV (Finale: E.D.U.)

G major, *Allegro*, 4/4, ♩=84

The exact form and nature of the finale may not have been decided until relatively late in the process of composition, but it must always have been intended to explore new territory. The sketch of theme A (folio 2v) bears the note 'for fuga'.[1] This intention is not realised by the counterpoint of certain variations (such as IV and XI); perhaps Elgar contemplated a big fugal finale, like Dvořák's. Instead, following Schumann's *Etudes symphoniques*, he invokes another finale topic, the march. Yet on one level XIV is indeed a variation, more so than X or XIII; indeed, since it presents all of the theme twice in new guises and with new counterpoints, it is two variations. The finale expands over broad paragraphs, incorporating references to two earlier variations; it concludes, after revision (see chapter 1), in a massive peroration which crowns the whole set (see table 4.1).

Earlier variations (II, XI, XII) have introductory material before the theme appears. In E.D.U. this is a sixteen-bar crescendo which adumbrates the later accelerando: two four-bar units are followed by a series of two-bar units while the harmony, above a tonic pedal, runs through the six triads available in G major.[2] The new motive (E), characterised by its sharp, almost military profile, culminates in the glorious assertion, *largamente*, at cue 62, where it acquires a rhythmic tail (♩♩♩) suggesting the first three notes of the theme (A). A accordingly makes itself felt, with a new spin on the familiar rhythm and a bold sally beyond the limits of the tonic, but it does not reach the falling sevenths; motive E seizes the initiative, and sallies abroad in a big irregular sequence (cue 63).[3] More

Table 4.1. *Outline of the finale*

Large formal units	Cue	Duration in bars	Smaller formal units
A: first complete variation	61	16	E (crescendo)
ABA form	62	23	A with E
	65	23	B with F
	68	19	A as Nimrod (quasi 3/2), 'grandioso'
B: second complete variation	70	8	E (crescendo)
AAB form	71	6	A with E
	72	7	'whistle'
	73	14	A as C.A.E. (section A)
	74	18	B with F
A': peroration and coda	76	25	E, B2, A (sevenths), *accelerando*, organ entry
	78	8	E, A (three-note), *sempre accelerando*, to Presto
	79	33	A (quasi 3/1)
	81	12	E
	82	25	A (five-note) and B2

largamente assertion (64) and another gesture based on A close off the first section with a strong dominant cadence.

Section B (cues 65–8) shrugs this modulation off, starting on the sub-dominant, C. It presents B1 in every bar, although none exactly matches the original intervals, and its impact lies as much in rhythm as contour, and in the rich texture of doubled thirds. Indeed, B1 quickly, if not immediately, sinks to the level of accompaniment to a new idea (F: cue 65, horns, clarinets, flutes), no less insistent in its rhythm, which blossoms to its own melodic climax at cue 66 and falls ravishingly to a half-close in E minor (66:4); its character is that of a folk-melody (Eric Sams is reminded of community singing), but it is saturated melodically by the protean falling scale, B2.[4]

The rest of section B is a reinforcing three-bar unit (66:5–7), and four two-bar units based on the ever-varying combination of B1 and F. The E minor ambience continues despite the insistent bass G (from cue 67). What follows closes off the first large unit of the finale, not by a return to the A/E combination, but by the reprise of the 'Nimrod' version of A, with its unique melodic alteration (here a′ where the theme would have b′); its triple metre, notated across the bar-lines (the 3/2 metre indicated by brackets), affects us like a strong current in a widening river. For ten bars 'Nimrod' is counterpointed by an extension of F; then a wild stringendo on the falling sevenths is cut off, without any closure.[5]

The second complete variation (cue 70) begins like the first, but the pace is hotter. The first crescendo picks up the harmonic position of 61:7, and is rescored with a mobile bass; the *largamente* (cue 71) is equivalent to cue 64 rather than 62. Theme A has one brief airing before another diversion, this time to a throbbing E♭. This could recall XIII, but we hear instead the whistle of C.A.E. on its own; it circles onto an A♮ to form a tritone with the bass, an eerie moment enhanced by skeletal percussion. The E♭ cadences into a restatement of the A section of C.A.E. in doubled note-values (cue 73), with all its seven strands plus rhythm E softly marked by trumpets and timpani (73:7).

Elgar then picks up the B/F combination in full flood, but where 'Nimrod' previously appeared he offers a swift dominant pedal crescendo (from cue 75). Thus both the complete variations within the finale are harmonically open-ended. Elgar, declaring that his original ending (seven bars on from cue 76) was adequate because the tonic key was exhausted (see p. 16), conveniently forgot that this was no deterrent to Mozart in opera finales.[6] The original ending reached a shuddering halt with material based on theme E: the penultimate chord is the augmented sixth which first appears at bar five of the theme. Jaeger and Richter recognised that the finale felt like an attempted summation finale cut off in its prime, perhaps because too much of it was devoted to reprise of earlier variations. Its bulk, in essence two long variations with insertions, required a greater peroration; it was a bar form (AA′B) without the B. Elgar's resistance to a 'grand finale' may result from the reticence which infected him at the climax of *Gerontius*; the rhetoric of drama and of nineteenth-century symphonism, after all, are closely akin.[7]

In the event he revived the tonic not only by strident allusions to other tonal areas (culminating in the grand E♭ chord of cue 82) but by two rhythmic devices, acceleration and variation in the larger metre.

Sketches of the ending show Elgar having difficulty with the notation, as he decided on the pacing of the closing bars. From cue 82 to the end, he expanded thirteen bars to fifteen, then crossed them through and further expanded them to seventeen and then to the final twenty-five.[8] Already cue 74 is *animando*; the sudden *piano* of 75 prepares a climax (beneath the swirling theme F and semiquaver figures, the rhythm of E sounds in violas, timpani, and horn). The huge accelerando from 76:11 reaches *presto* at cue 79 (o =84 – four times the original speed). Elgar had already introduced 'Nimrod' in its original triple metre; from cue 69 he drives forward in quintuple metre: there are three effective bars of 5/2, the second marked by the *rf* in mid-bar (69:3). An extra beat (marked *fffz*) is thrown in, so that the half-bar before cue 70 and cue 70 itself are both heard as down-beats. At cue 79 the first three bars are bracketed to mark a triple hypermeter; this prevails for eleven 'bars' of 3/1 (79–81), whereupon the next four bars are bracketed to restore a duple hypermeter. The grandeur of the result is itself eloquent, and arises so naturally that it is astonishing that it was not always part of the design; the optional organ part, confined to the new section, adds another dimension to the sound.[9]

E.D.U. is the composer himself, mainly in unbuttoned mood. Newman calls it 'a superb outburst, remarkable both for its clever theme-weaving and its glorious colour' (this, of course, with the revised ending). Powell says that when he first played it to her 'hilarity knew no bounds. E.E. shouted with laughter. But I had not then grasped who E.D.U. was and I remember thinking what a determined and forceful person this must be . . .' (the penny only dropped later). Elgar called the finale 'bold and vigorous', adding that it was written 'at a time when friends were dubious and generally discouraging as to the composer's musical future'. This may be disingenuous, but the continuation rings true: 'this variation is merely to show what E.D.U. . . . . intended to do', or, as Powell puts it, he 'delighted in what he had done and he knew he had done it well'. Allusions to Alice and Jaeger, 'two great influences on the life and art of the composer, are entirely fitting to the intention of the piece' (*MFPW*). The last presentation of the theme concludes with the five-note shape ending on the dominant (82:2–83); the counterpoint (violins) describes, in G minor, the opening shape of Elgar's First Symphony in A♭, a work he connected with 'a *massive* hope in the future'.[10] Also ending on the dominant, this shape has potential for signifying optimism and perhaps (bearing Elgar's remark in mind) unfinished business; although it has also been traced to the Mendelssohn quotation in XIII.[11] These points have some bearing on rhetorical or enigmatic interpretations of the set as a whole (see chapter 5).

The grand design 1: order of the variations

The sketches include no fewer than five lists of the variations. The earliest (see table 1.1) is not intended to indicate a final ordering; the remaining four are combined in table 4.2. The first two columns (2–3) are derived from a loose sheet of paper, now attached to a sketch-leaf (folio 32) containing two more tables on the verso (the basis of columns 4–5).[12] There is no indication of their chronological relationship. In order to form any hypothesis I have assumed without evidence that the lists gradually approach the final version (appended in column 6), with one exception; column 4, headed 'old list', and column 5, new (presumably) in relation to column 4, are in a clear chronological relationship. Apart from the words 'theme' and 'finale', the loose sheet consists only of numbers, so the identification of variations in table 4.2 must be treated with caution; columns 4 and 5 are aligned with a set of friends' initials. The 'new' list is close to the final order; but B.G.N. is marked 10, replaced by 9, although these places are also occupied by 'Dorabella' and 'Nimrod'.

If table 4.2 is correct, the opening sequence of three variations was quickly established, and W.M.B. soon followed as IV. The migration of R.P.A. to V (column 4) settled the final positions as far as 'Nimrod'. The rest reveals particular uncertainty for G.R.S., who is not included in the 'new list'. An apparently firm intention to place B.G.N. last before the finale was finally overturned by the decision to use (***) at this point; B.G.N. went to XII, but was reconsidered for X or IX. 'Dorabella' originally appears rather late for an intermezzo (column 2); her relation to 'Nimrod' varies, although column 2 has the final version. It is also notable that the variations connected by *attacca* (R.P.A. to 'Ysobel', W.N. to 'Nimrod', B.G.N. to (***)) are established by the 'old list', whose only difference from the final version is the order of 'Dorabella' and G.R.S. Some reasons for the decisions Elgar finally took may be deduced from consideration of the musical evidence, but it is clear that the 'grand design' emerged late in the conception of *Variations*.

Table 4.2. *Possible reordering of variations*

1	2 memo [C.A.E.?]	3 memo [E.E.]	4 fo. 32v 'old list'	5 fo. 32v [new list]	6 Completed score
	Theme				
I	C.A.E.				
II	H.D.S-P.				
III	R.B.T.				
IV	Ysobel	W.M.B.			
V	G.R.S.	G.R.S.	R.P.A.		
VI	***	***	Ysobel		
VII	W.M.B.	Ysobel	Troyte		
VIII	W.N.	Troyte	W.N.		
IX	Troyte	W.N.	Nimrod	Nimrod/B.G.N.	Nimrod
X	R.P.A.	Dorabella	G.R.S.	Dorabella	Dorabella
XI	Nimrod	Nimrod	Dorabella	?	G.R.S.
XII	Dorabella	R.P.A.	B.G.N.	?	B.G.N.
XIII	B.G.N.	B.G.N.	***	***	***
XIV	E.D.U.	E.D.U.	E.D.U.	[blank]	E.D.U.

The grand design 2: unity, tonality, and rhetoric

The demonstration of musical unity, or even consistency, by way of thematic analysis may seem redundant in variations; two sections (X and
XIII) have to be scoured for references to the theme, but it is otherwise
ubiquitous. Moreover, tonal coherence is obvious, the variations depart-
ing only slightly from G minor and G major, with one tonal non sequitur
(VIII–IX–X) expressing an indirect key-relation (I–♭VI, here G–E♭)
well established in nineteenth-century music.

As finally ordered, *Variations* is easily segmented by key into three
units. Units 1 (theme, I–IV) and 3 (X–XIV) are based on parallel modes
of the tonic, and unit 2 (V–IX), with one variation in the tonic, is based
on C major, C minor, and its relative E♭. But within each unit, however
defined, unity of key makes a lesser effect than divergence of character
(as in Brahms's 'Haydn' variations, all of which, however, are in the parallel modes of B♭). The three-unit pattern may inspire comparison to

59

sonata form (exposition, development, recapitulation), but only as a metaphor: *Variations* is not unified like a single movement, lacking either a committed departure from the home key, or a correspondingly articulated return. The subdominant group in unit 2 is more episodic than architectural, and the return to G in VIII is premature, followed by another departure ('Nimrod') and another return: both returns (W.N. and 'Dorabella'), lacking brass and percussion like nearly all the G-major music before the finale, are too delicate, or playful, to bear the rhetorical weight of recapitulation.

Elgar had in mind widely divergent musical, as well as human, personalities; in adhering to the pitches of his theme, he presents them in a way suggesting variety as a rhetorical objective. It remains tempting to continue the traditional analytic exercise of seeking out significant similarities, especially as variety satisfies most in a context which seems coherent. Within unit 1 there is already a sense of departure and return, expressed by rhythmic properties of theme A (see Ex. 2.3); IV is the same as the theme minus the rests. However, I–IV also depart from the theme in ways for which the path back is only found in V. IV presents the characteristic rhythm at four times its original speed, whereas V restores the tempo and mood of the theme, despite being in 12/8 and C minor: the full, quiet orchestration and enlivening of the theme by counterpoint evoke the passion (here more restrained) of C.A.E., and beneath new material, A is heard in the original 4/4 (in the sketch Elgar used two time-signatures). This analysis brings Richard Arnold, son of a poet, close to C.A.E., herself a poet.

From this might arise an alternative subdivision: unit 1 (theme and I–V), entirely in minor keys but for its central variation, unit 2 (VI–X) entirely in major keys. Within unit 2, 'Ysobel' provides the first in a series of affectively varied intermezzi in which the first part of the theme no longer assumes pride of place. When B appears in 'Ysobel', it is close to its original character, and B forms the main thematic material of 'Troyte', which crudely reduces A to its rhythm in the ostinato. With VIII (W.N.), A regains its shape, but is transformed as it develops by replication of the first four notes, without the inverted, rising third of the theme's bar 2, and without the falling sevenths; the B section of W.N. is again closer, in its rise and fall, to B in the theme. In fact 'Nimrod' stands out within the middle unit (however defined) not only by tempo, character, and key, but by its concentration on the primal thematic material.

At first the subdivisions are reinforced by metronome markings, with variation V returning to the speed of the theme and C.A.E., and II–IV linked proportionately (II and IV: whole bar = 72; III: beat = 144). In the middle, W.N. and 'Nimrod' 'should', according to the markings, have the same quaver value. But towards the end, with variations measured at 80, 100, 76, and (finale) 84, no clear system can be perceived; moreover, Elgar himself did not observe these relations in performance (see chapter 6).

Elgar clearly did not juxtapose variations for social (programmatic) reasons, such as the piano trio combination, E.D.U., B.G.N., and H.D.S-P. Perhaps G.R.S. was displaced at V (table 4.2, columns 2–3) by the C minor of R.P.A. because, for the time being, Elgar felt the tonic would be exhausted. Three variations in C provide relief from the tonic (table 4.2 suggests that Elgar quickly established the 'Ysobel'–'Troyte' pairing); W.N. restores G major in a new pastoral mood. Near the centre, 'Nimrod' stands furthest from the tonic. When placed next to R.P.A. (columns 2–3), the E♭ major of 'Nimrod' was naturally juxtaposed to its relative, C minor. The 'old list' followed it with the closer form of the tonic, G minor, and cruelly destroys the mood with G.R.S.; in the final version, Elgar surrounds it with G major, *attacca* from W.N., and followed after a silence by 'Dorabella', so that the remoteness of E♭ major becomes a positive contribution to the characterisation. The rest of the cycle is dictated by the vitality of contrast: delicate 'Dorabella', animal spirits (XI), refined sentiment (XII), and the inner contrasts of XIII. Overall, it may appear that tonality as a means of ordering is tempered by something as indefinable as 'what feels right'.

Nevertheless, the final ordering allows the closing stages to enfold two G minor variations within the G major of the intermezzi, X and XIII; the major mode is then confirmed in the finale. Some sense of overall form is derived from the minor–major movement of the theme itself, in which G major (section B) is cancelled by section A′ but restored by its final chord ('tierce de Picardie', as Elgar noted in a sketch). This promise of G major, treated similarly in II, is suppressed by III and IV; V begins the group in C. After the solid exposition of the tonic modes in unit 1, unit 2 is more fluid, less directionally clear, as befits a middle (every variation is a development, but here is an analogy with a development *section*). But the uncertainty marking any metaphorical recapitulation is indicative of tangled hierarchies: it could be X, restoring the tonic, XI, restoring the shape of the theme, or XII, restoring the periodic structure of the theme and its elegiac mood. None of the later variations could function as a finale; none of them, moreover, seems to point strongly (like a sonata retransition) towards a resolution.

As the cycle progresses, systems of tonality, climax-control, and degree of similarity to the theme, which might be presumed to lend coherence to a long structure, operate separately rather than in concinnity. Restoration of the tonic ('Dorabella') is accompanied by the furthest departure from the contour, phraseology, and tonal organisation of the theme. When a new start is signified in XI, with its return to the primitive intervals of the theme, Dan's orgy of splashing rudely confuses A and B. These are carefully separated once more in XII, which also restores the ternary design of the theme and its stepping bass; but as with C.A.E., the period corresponding to theme B is *not* in G major. Thus XII, like a reprise, stabilises memories of the theme as the cycle approaches its end, while continuing to present new tonal and melodic elements.

From the formal viewpoint, XIII remains enigmatic. Tenuously connected to the theme, it forms another intermezzo before the finale; but in its continually frustrated design, its slender orchestration, and the passages on chords of A♭ and E♭ – far longer than the tonic sections and a challenge to the hegemony of G major – it has neither the self-contained nature of an intermezzo, nor the conviction of a reprise. Indeed, but for a final, barely audible major third, it might have reversed the progression implied in the theme by going from major to minor. A large-scale formal analogy within the design as a whole might be a troubled recitative for a single character before the resolution of an all-embracing operatic finale. It is noteworthy in this connection that XIII is one of the variations joined by sound to another. These links – the extra bars between the theme and C.A.E., the way V only stops with the first note of VI, and the mood-changing held note from VIII to IX – are rhetorical and musical, but not programmatic; there are no especial personal connections between Arnold and Miss Fitton (V–VI), Miss Norbury and Jaeger (VIII–IX), or Nevinson (XII) and Lady Mary (XIII) to explain the linking of their variations. The last such link, from XII to XIII, rather serves to mark the different worlds to which they belong.[13] The removal of the last bar of a 'complete' XII ends it on a question mark, in mid-air; the answer to the question was given earlier (52:3), when the same music was completed by the restoration of the theme and bass. The *attacca* to XIII deprives us of further reassurance, a deliberate non sequitur to prepare for the fundamental incoherence of XIII as a whole, and a tactic designed to sharpen the appetite for closure eventually satisfied by the finale. Elgar's rhetorical, and thus formal, skill is as apparent even in so simple a matter as the uses to which he puts continuity of sound between certain sections.

On the face of it, the patterns just outlined are not conspicuously coherent or satisfying; and in performance, in Elgar's time, the work may well have been interrupted for applause, severely qualifying any links across otherwise unconnected variations. But it is important not to interpret patterns synchronically, viewed in space, as it were, rather than time; and we cannot be sure that Elgar approved of audience intervention. Certainly he took trouble to dispose his variations to best effect. If we consider the result diachronically, and thus rhetorically, it suggests an intelligible and well co-ordinated set of departures and returns, of beginnings, middles, and ends, which find completion only in the strongest beginning and ending, both in the finale. For this reason weak presentations of the tonic major – in the theme, playfully in III, isolated in VIII, not a variation in X, questioned by XIII – collectively strengthen the whole work, and allow the initial crescendos of the finale to establish for the first time a tonic major of real mass.

5

The enigmas

This chapter is a selective guide to published 'solutions' to 'the enigma'. There are certainly more; some, indeed, that I know of have merited no more than a passing mention. Comprehensive treatment would fill a book and, since interest in the question shows no sign of abating, I expect to be out of date on publication. I shall propose no new solution, nor try to fathom the solvers' psychology, beyond remarking that it may lead to illnesses dangerous to scholars, such as selective quotation.

Some solutions separate, and some mingle, the positivistic and the interpretative. The first type tries to trace sources for the conception of the theme and the portraits of friends, basing interpretation on verifiable facts. The second is more concerned to find an inner meaning which may have formed no part of Elgar's thinking on the critical October weekend of 1898. Since the word 'enigma' was only added to the score a month or so before the first performance, 'the enigma' may have been a retrospective act of interpretation by the composer himself, followed up over the years in letters, interviews, annotations (including *MFPW*), and musical reminiscences, notably in *The Music Makers*. On the other hand, it is occasionally proposed that the 'enigma' was a joke.[1]

It was certainly effective publicity. Unlike Potter (see p. 22), Elgar was not writing *à la manière de. . .* those who really were 'asses enough to compose', and the identities of his friends, while sufficient to justify 'enigma' as a subtitle, would be unknown and of little interest to an audience; so a more wide-ranging mystery was immediately published. Elgar at first appeared ready to confirm a correct solution, but not to be cross-examined; later he may have decided always to say 'no'. Richard Powell, married to 'Dorabella', was not the only person to suggest *Auld lang syne*, and when Elgar denied it, Dora loyally opposed her husband; later she tearfully confided to Roger Fiske that Elgar must have lied.[2] Perhaps, when the puzzle was not quickly resolved, Elgar became embarrassed by the solution, either because of its contrived complexity or, on the contrary, because of its banality. By the 1920s Op. 36, a well-established part of the modern orchestral repertoire, had been followed by greater orchestral works – symphonies, concertos, *Falstaff* – and a flood of well-merited honours. Elgar's notoriously thin skin may have itched at the prospect of a popular melody being irrevocably associated with his first recognised masterpiece. Or, maybe, far from being amusing or ingenious, the enigma hid feelings too deep for words, too tender for public scrutiny. As Basil Maine observed, 'Elgar's greatest wisdom lies in this, that he knows how to keep his own counsel.'[3]

Nevertheless, we have the composer's word that there *was* an enigma. I make no apology for quoting again the note for the first performance, nor for numbering the sections to connect them to the subsequent discussion.

[i] It *is* true that I have sketched for their amusement and mine, the idiosyncrasies of fourteen of my friends, not necessarily musicians; but this is a personal matter, and need not have been mentioned publicly. [ii] The Variations should stand simply as a 'piece' of music. [iii] The Enigma I will not explain – [iv] its 'dark saying' must be left unguessed, [v] and I warn you that the connexion between the Variations and the Theme is often of the slightest texture; [vi] further, through and over the whole set another and larger theme 'goes', but is not played . . . So the principal Theme never appears, even as in some late dramas – e.g., Maeterlinck's 'L'Intruse' and 'Les sept Princesses' – the chief character is never on the stage.[4]

This passage raises a ripe mixture of unanswerable questions, not least why the composer indulged in obfuscation as early as 1899. These points emerge: (i) Elgar distinguished the enigma from the identities of his friends, most of which he later published. Presumably this separation applies equally to XIII, although enigma-crackers have devoted attention to the identity behind (***) (see below). But if it was a private matter, why did Elgar mention it publicly at all? (ii) That Op. 36 stands 'as a piece of music' reminds us that there is no *need*, from the aesthetic rather than psychological point of view, to find a solution. (iii) Nowadays the force of 'I will', the future imperative, may be weaker than in Elgar's time.[5] His determination not to be drawn was maintained to the end, even within his intimate circle. (iv) From this it follows that anything purporting to be a 'solution' must indicate at least the nature of the 'dark saying', or even identify it. (v) This seems to be a non sequitur: the issue of form is ostensibly unconnected to the enigma. (vi) Another and larger theme 'goes' (Elgar's 'scare quotes') over the whole set; the protagonist is never on stage.[6] It follows from this that any 'solution' must fulfil certain criteria:

(1) The solution must unveil a dark saying (although the composer said it 'must be left unguessed').

(2) The solution must find 'another and larger theme' which *goes* over the whole set.

Dora Powell explained that there are two mysteries, distinguishing the enigma and its 'dark saying' from the 'larger theme': 'the notion that it could be anything other than a tune is relatively modern . . . Elgar made it perfectly clear to us when the work was being written that the Enigma was concerned with a tune'.[7] But a 'dark saying' cannot simply be a tune. The 'larger theme' might be a tune, or it might be metaphorical, such as the 'theme of friendship'. Mrs Powell provides two more criteria: as early as November 1899 Elgar told her 'It is so well known that it is extraordinary that no-one has spotted it.' This point was later reinforced by Troyte Griffith who offered *God Save the King* and was told 'of course not . . . but it is extraordinary no-one has found it'. To Dora alone he said (at an undisclosed later date) 'I thought that you of all people would guess it'.[8] From this follow criteria (3) and (4):

(3) The solution involves well-known music, or at least something well known.

(4) It must be clear why Dora Penny 'of all people' should guess it.

Few solutions even try to meet all these criteria, which themselves are open to varying interpretations. The 'dark saying' (1), assuming it existed in some form in Elgar's mind, might not be subject to capture by another. The editors of the *Complete Edition* pour cold water on the concept.[9] That it might be an identifiable saying (see below) is only an assumption; the 'saying' might be essentially musical, and not translatable into words. The 'larger theme' (2) was referred to by Elgar in conversation with Dora Penny as 'it'; yet she was emphatic that a well-known tune was involved (3). How this tune might fit into a solution is unclear, and this criterion has led to more bizarre explanations than any other, many based on entirely false premises. It has often been remarked that no musical theme can ever literally 'go over the whole set'. Elgar's comment (4) may be personal to Dora, but he may have meant only that anyone in the immediate circle of friends might be expected to guess.

To these criteria we may tentatively add (5): the 'solution' should take into account the characteristic falling sevenths of bars 3–4. Elgar himself drew especial attention to these with the cryptic observation: 'The drop of a seventh in the Theme (bars 3 and 4) should be observed.'[10] Observed must mean more than merely performed, which might be the case if he had been referring to a dynamic marking; but it could be an analytical comment on what becomes of the sevenths in the variations. Any solution which neglects this critical point in the theme, however, may be suspect. In what follows I have attempted some classification, but the most interesting 'solutions' are those which turn up under more than one heading.[11]

The 'source' melody

The object of this type of 'solution' is to impugn the originality of Elgar's theme. What was 'on his brain' to shape his improvisation on 21 October 1898? What lies hidden within his own melody? The host of tempting possibilities includes earlier Elgar; Young proposes the Gavotte Op. 10 no. 3.[12] Unfortunately, most 'sources' share with the theme only the most commonplace of musical materials. The opening shape, falling thirds separated by a rising fourth, was no stranger to Elgar's music. It appears at a critical point in *The Black Knight*, the last repetition of the line 'He beholds his children die' (vocal score p. 61; the key is E♭), a context inescapably melancholy, albeit in the major mode. The first three notes of A appear with equal programmatic significance in *Caractacus* (vocal score p. 179), as the Emperor spares the Britons: 'Young warrior, *clasp thy bride.*' The first major-mode music in *Caractacus*, as in *Variations*, uses the first four notes of B1, significantly doubled in thirds (the vocal entry, p. 3: 'Watchmen, alert!'). Near the end, at 'Thro' all the ling'ring hours' (p. 182), Brian Trowell notes the anticipation of the contour of theme B, in triple time.[13] John Rollett's derivation of theme B from the introductory 'Meditation' to *The Light of Life* (vocal score p. 3, at letter E) is less compelling.[14]

These instances could all be attributed to the composer's habits; outside 'sources' require more explanation. Westrup suggests, from a work dear to Elgar, the setting of 'Eli, Eli, lama sabachthani' (Lord, Lord, why hast thou forsaken me?) in Bach's *St Matthew Passion*, although few intervals correspond.[15] Another melodic connection is the *Benedictus* of Stanford's Requiem, which Elgar certainly knew.[16] Also with a religious connotation, Ulrik Skouenborg proposes a complicated derivation from the first of Brahms's *Vier ernste Gesänge*, setting the dark words 'and if I have not charity'.[17] Ben Kingdon tries to find the *Dies Irae* plainchant, familiar not only from the church but from its use in several nineteenth-century works, lurking within the theme; a good candidate for being 'so well known', and no less dark a saying.[18]

Other proposals lack this 'dark' dimension. A competition in the *Saturday Review* (1953) turned up ideas of manifest irrelevance, except for the slow movement of Beethoven's *Pathétique* sonata, whose relation to 'Nimrod' was intentional, and signalled by Elgar himself (*MFPW*).[19] The many-sided solution of Theodore van Houten depends in part on the occurrence of the opening intervals in the chorus of *Rule, Britannia*, customarily sung to 'never, never'.[20] This is certainly well enough known; and the main charm of this solution is that Dora Penny 'of all people' should indeed have recognised it. The duodecimal penny coin, in use until 1970, showed the figure of Britannia on the reverse side to the monarch.

The link between the theme and a passage in the slow movement of Mozart's 'Prague' Symphony K. 504 was widely publicised by Joseph Cooper (who managed to involve B1, but not the falling sevenths: see appendix). Jerrold Northrop Moore supported this by retelling the story of 21 October 1898 to imply that Elgar might have wandered into memories of Mozart until finding something of his own.[21] For a composer to begin a piece by reference to an admired model, or something with potential which could be done better or differently, is perfectly normal; there can be little doubt, for instance, that Elgar's Second Symphony is indebted to the scheme of Brahms's Third. Moore notes the central place of Mozart in Elgar's musical pantheon, and specifically in his training, making it natural that 'when he found himself in a creative

wilderness . . . his mind should return as if by instinct to Mozart . . .'
Moore links the 'Prague' to Op. 36 in other ways, including a performance in Leeds shortly after *Caractacus*, on 7 October, attended by
the Elgars. But while Elgar may have suffered one of his depressive
cycles, normal after the production of a major work, he could hardly be
said, with the 'Gordon' symphony 'possessing' his mind, to have been in
a creative wilderness (and Beethoven, rather than Mozart, was used by
Jaeger to get Elgar out of creative despair).[22]

The Mozart theory involves neither a dark saying nor 'another and
larger theme'; nor does it meet the 'Dorabella' criteria, for the 'Prague'
is surely not so well known as to be considered obvious. But in any case
this type of 'solution' solves nothing. Many examples hang by the
merest thread, the source coinciding with the theme, in some cases, by
as few as three notes; given the limitations of the seven-note scale, these
seem insufficient to bear intertextual weight. But, more importantly,
Elgar never implied that the mystery concerned the actual notes of the
theme; these solutions are solving a different kind of problem and
(except when part of a multifaceted solution) they fail the test of rele-
vance.

Other ways to make a theme

On a simple level, the melody might indeed be original, but derived from
word-setting. The lack of a down-beat, or rather the relative weakness of
the first accented 'syllable' (second beat of bar 1), suits poetic lines and,
indeed, the composer's name, a point often made.

Brian Trowell suggests that playing the theme under a tonic pedal
'makes unusual but perfectly good Elgarian invertible two-part counterpoint with the Enigma theme over its bass'; if the texture is transposed to
E minor, this pedal reads 'E.E.'[23] It was perhaps Dora who first referred
to the composer as E.E.; Elgar sometimes signed himself with octave Es;
Jaeger once jokingly addressed him as 'the octave . . . you SPHYNX!',
probably an allusion to Schumann's *Carnaval*, and used the initials (with
how much intention to hint we cannot tell) when protesting to Dora that
he could not reveal the secret.[24] Trowell also points out that the tune can
be underlaid with the words, strangely misquoted from Tasso, which
Elgar wrote at the end of the score, and which constitute a dark enough

Ex. 5.1 The theme underlaid with the Tasso text

Bra - mo   as - sai,   po - co spe - ro,   nul - la chieg - gio

saying: 'Bramo assai, poco spero, nulla chieggio' (I desire much, I hope little, I ask nothing: see Ex. 5.1).[25]

A tempting avenue leads to ciphers, although the short interval (three days) between conception and the commitment implied by mentioning the existence of the Variations to Jaeger makes elaborate precompositional calculation unlikely.[26] Nevertheless, this would not prevent cryptograms appearing within Elgar's retrospective interpretation of his own work. The musical ciphers most likely to have appealed to Elgar are Schumann's, such as ABEGG, and ASCH in *Carnaval*. Our leading musical cryptographer, Eric Sams, came in behind *Auld lang syne* as the hidden melody, but not as counterpoint; rather, he suggests the tune is enciphered in the texture of both themes A and B (including parts of the harmony), the third bar, with the falling seventh, having particular significance (thus meeting criterion (5)). Moreover, his ingenious embedding technique can run through the whole set, although it leaves many notes unaccounted for.[27] Equally 'good' results could be obtained from any pentatonic melody, such as *Loch Lomond*, which incidentally is hardly worse counterpoint than *Auld lang syne* (see appendix). As for criterion (4), Sams points out that Elgar tried out a cipher on Dora Penny.[28] But she was unable to read it; she of all people could *not* be expected to work out this one. None of this shows that Sams is wrong. Van Houten supports his own theory by a spectacular display of anagrams, and also proposes that R.B.T. is an acronym: R[ule] B[ri] T[annia], which might explain why his initials appear on music possibly first intended for Atkins (see p. 15).

Parrott proposed Bach as a larger theme because his name is embedded in the theme at its extremities: B (German B♭), H (B♮).[29] But in between, C appears before A. Marshall A. Portnoy also makes Bach 'the answer', without revealing any dark saying.[30] Two other ciphers depend on transposition of the theme to A minor. For Geoffrey Poole the theme yields 'Caroline Alice' (i.e. Mrs Elgar), although imperfectly.[31] Christopher Seaman uses the same cipher, but by including bass notes where the violins rest he reveals a dedication to the composer's daughter: 'A Carice'.[32] If so, it is strange that Elgar never told her, or if he did, strange that she remained silent and encouraged Powell to believe in the tune theory – although she is reported, on seeing the Ashton ballet, to have said of its portrayals: 'they were all exactly like that . . . And I never liked any of them, except Troyte.'[33]

It seems virtually certain that the theme, whatever led Elgar to call it 'Enigma', represents the composer, an idea proposed as early as 1900 by the perceptive critic of the *Manchester Guardian*, Arthur Johnstone. On 10 and 25 October 1901 Elgar signed letters to Dora Penny with the first notes of theme A, and contrasted her cheerful 'variation' with his own glum theme, in one case marked 'unideal', in the other *mesto* (gloomy).[34] Identification of Elgar with the theme is supported by Eric Sams; at least this idea does not suffer from the main obstacle to revelation by cipher, which is the sheer speed at which the essentials of the Variations emerged. Ciphers are particularly difficult to reconcile with the story of 21 October 1898.

Counterpoint: the hidden tune

Further search in earlier works of Elgar yields interesting results. Brian Trowell locates the first six notes of the bass (bars 1–3) in *Caractacus*, in the introduction and the fugal section 'Comrades, comrades, firm and fearless', a call to arms and by analogy to artistic solidarity.[35] Rollett proposes the introduction ('Meditation') from *The Light of Life*, since the theme of Christ's restoration of light (vocal score p. 4, letter G) fits at least the first two bars of the theme so long as its own harmony is used; without harmony, the counterpoint extends further (see appendix). For criterion (3) he notes that 'Meditation', often performed on its own, was well known to Elgar's friends.[36] Trying Boyce's *Heart of Oak* (like *Auld lang syne*, changed to the minor), Charles Ross shows only a poor correspondence with the diatonic chord-progression underlying the theme. More interestingly, he notes that the Mendelssohn quotation in XIII and the passage *not* in quotation marks which follows (56:7–10) correspond to part of the same song.[37]

One reading of Elgar's specification suggests 'another theme' as *counterpoint* to the original theme. Those who prefer other approaches, such as Westrup and Poole, convince themselves that Elgar never implied this.[38] His mind could certainly work that way, witness his combination of the National Anthem with the 5/4 waltz from Tchaikovsky's *Pathé-tique*.[39] And this type of solution has historic authority. In 1900 *The Musical Times* reported: 'In connection with these much discussed Variations, Mr Elgar tells us that the heading "Enigma" is justified by the fact that it is possible to add another phrase, which is quite familiar, above the original theme that he has written.' R. J. Buckley in the first monograph on Elgar (1905), claiming that much of his material represents 'actual words addressed to the writer', says: 'The theme is a counterpoint on some well-known melody which is never heard.'[40] The first important 'solution', devised about 1920 and published within a few months of Elgar's death, was that of Richard Powell; it is essentially that the theme (not the variations) 'goes' with *Auld lang syne*, an idea which obstinately refuses to die.[41] Wisely, Powell sought a familiar melody 'that will not, at first sight, appear to fit any too well'. He puts the first strain of the song into the parallel minor, although he might equally have followed Elgar by presenting theme A in the major. Diana McVeagh points out that 'by leaving [*Auld lang syne*] in the major, in the relative key of B♭, it makes a more credible counterpoint' (see appendix).[42]

A. H. Fox Strangways added in a note to Powell's article that the characteristic dotted rhythm of *Auld lang syne*, missing from the theme, is prominent in the finale ('F', from cue 65, the new counterpoint to B).[43] Later, Fox Strangways rehearsed various objections, adding a report of Elgar's denial: '*Auld lang syne* won't do': (a) the triviality of the tune is an insufficient objection but (b) it is hardly a *larger* tune (*sic*; Elgar said theme). Finally (c), it 'does not go properly even with the original theme'. But as Roger Fiske observed (1969), 'the remarkable thing is not how badly the tune fits, but how well'.[44] And '*Auld lang syne* won't do' does not suggest that the *nature* of Powell's search was wrong.

As we have already seen, however, Eric Sams found another way to envelop *Auld lang syne* in the theme. Derek Hudson improves Powell's counterpoint and fits *Auld lang syne* against the slower variations except, significantly, XIII.[45] Most of the proposed counterpoints simply will not pass scrutiny – and *God Save the Queen*, which Elgar also rejected, is no worse than most (see appendix).[46] One might argue that, since Elgar did not intend the tunes actually to be heard together, the counterpoint does not need to be simon-pure. But after so many years of searching, any solution worthy of belief requires something as clean and effective as the counterpoint in the composition itself; otherwise how can one rate one dubious combination above another? Epitomising the argument from a musical standpoint, Tovey dismissed the *Auld lang syne* counterpoint as 'not nearly good enough', adding 'any composer designing a counterpoint to the melody would be practically certain to make it fit the bass also'.[47]

A larger theme

A musician may find it easier to believe that the 'larger theme' is a metaphor, in which case, however, it becomes confused with the 'dark saying', something Elgar's wording seems to exclude. Dora Powell speaks dismissively of certain interpretations ('the Line of the Malvern Hills, the Personality of the Composer, and the Chromatic Scale'), although the second has some mileage.[48] Richard Powell's paradigmatic solution was reached by way of an abstract theme: a work dedicated not to persons in the public eye but to friends pictured within led him to *Auld lang syne*. In the second monograph on the composer (1906) Ernest Newman attempted no solution, but in 1939 he supported the possibility of 'friendship'; later Percy M. Young declares this unequivocally to be 'the idea behind the Enigma set'.[49]

Sir Thomas Browne, in *Religio Medici*, wrote: 'There are wonders in true affection: it is a body of *Enigmas*, mysteries, and riddles . . .', a passage Elgar, who owned a copy, will have relished.[50] But almost any prior use of the word 'enigma' might be recruited for the hunt. Ian Parrott reminds us that the Greek and Vulgate texts of St Paul's first letter to the Corinthians (XIII.12) use 'enigma' where the Authorised Version has seeing 'through a glass, darkly' (other translations refer more directly to a mirror).[51] The passage is concerned with maturing, and is embedded within his sermon on charity (love: friendship). But van Houten not only maintains that Britannia 'herself' is portrayed within the music, but that the larger, abstract theme, developed with a wealth of cross-reference, is patriotism; as with *Auld lang syne*, therefore,

Rule, Britannia combines a well-known melody with a larger meta-phorical theme.

In 1959 Jerrold Northrop Moore proposed an alternative secular metaphor. Adducing the use of the theme in *The Music Makers*, he suggests that Op. 36 'represents Elgar's – and every artist's – search for self-discovery and self-expression through his art'.[52] For Moore, the statement made by Op. 36 is 'purely aesthetic'; *Variations* 'is a piece of music whose subject-matter is music, and ultimately all of art'. Elgar's own statement that the theme 'expressed when written . . . my sense of the loneliness of the artist' was made in a note to *The Music Makers*, in which the theme is associated with 'desolate streams' (a connection underlined by Westrup). For Moore, the work expresses a progress from this mood of introspective isolation (E.E.) to the confident finale (E.D.U.). A spiritual element derived from *The Light of Life* is combined by Rollett with an idealised autobiography: 'The transition from darkness to light is the essence of the Oratorio, just as the transition from loneliness to confident assertiveness is the essence of the *Variations*.'[53] Rainer Fanselau proposes that the self-characterisation is a motive for using the organ, and an indication that the composer intended to write great sacred works.[54] These ideas have the seductiveness of the unknowable, but receive some support from Brian Trowell's analysis of the Tasso quotation.[55] Nevertheless, the alleged discouragement of Elgar's friends after *Caractacus* makes their celebration in a new work either ironic or unlikely. There was discouragement from the publisher, but not from Elgar's friend in Novello's, Jaeger; Burley insisted that 'there was never a time after, at any rate, 1892 when his friends were less than optimistic and encouraging', although of course it matters psychologically how Elgar actually felt.[56] Hindsight might suggest that the appearance of the opening theme of the First Symphony in the closing bars of the revised coda reflects back into Op. 36 the idea of hope (see p. 57); his reluctance later to discuss the enigma reflects his subsequent pessimism.

Individual variations

Attempts have been made to explain things by reference to individual variations, which are sometimes said, without any warrant from contemporary documentation or sketches, to have preceded the theme. With

Beethoven's *Pathétique* possibly in Elgar's mind, Westrup hazarded but dismissed the notion that 'Nimrod' preceded the theme; and also that the work took off from Elgar's frustrated love for dogs (Alice did not like them), with G.R.S. the first musical idea.[57] This started a hare which Parrott has enthusiastically pursued, originating the theme in the remarkable vigour and accuracy of Sinclair's organ pedalling: 47:2–3, equal quavers in the bass, looks like a Bach pedal exercise.[58] That G.R.S. came late in order of composition makes this less likely, even if Dan's bark was a play on the composer's name. That this is the simplest form of the notes does not imply that it must have preceded the theme conceptually. That the theme starts with rests on strong beats may be unusual, and may indeed make it suitable as a countersubject, but in itself Elgar's idea does not go far beyond models like the finale of the 'Prague' (again!), or the opening of Beethoven's Fifth.

Most approaches by way of individual variations focus on XIII. It is clear from documentary sources, including Elgar's draft for *MFPW*, that (***) is Lady Mary Lygon, but less clear why is it not called L.M.L., as in the sketches, and why, since Lygon was not yet at sea, it includes the Mendelssohn quotation (see p. 52). Moore suggests that following the announcement of her voyage, it must have been revised; but from what?[59] As it stands, most of the variation is devoted to imagery identified (with Elgar's encouragement) as marine. While accepting the dedication, Lygon may have declined, for whatever reason, to be publicly identified, or even lightly disguised ('Lady' was not her name). Elgar wrote to her about the variation in a friendly spirit while she was abroad, but while finishing *Variations* he also dedicated *Three Characteristic Pieces* (piano version) to her, urging Jaeger on 24 March 1899 to get the title-page ready before she sailed: is this because she knew the variation was not really hers?[60]

Rosa Burley and Ernest Newman believed that (***) concealed the identity of someone else, whom both refused to name.[61] Kennedy followed Newman's lead by pointing to an *amour* at Leipzig, where Elgar went in 1883, later identified as Helen Weaver, suggesting that this fiancée of Elgar's youth was also the love of his life.[62] Identification of Helen as (***) and as the secret dedicatee of the violin concerto ('Here is enshrined the soul of . . . .') received striking support from Wulstan Atkins.[63] This interpretation is persuasive, although those sceptical

Ex. 5.2 The theme in the sketch of C.A.E.

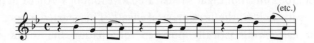

about the expressive force of the variation might point out that inside knowledge may have caused Ernest Newman to change his view of it (see p. 53). If the penultimate variation referred to a lost love, darkness enters the enigma. The theory is supported by Elgar's perhaps deliberate mistake concerning the date of Lady Mary's departure. Burley, claiming the evocation of a seascape was 'accidental', even queried whether the quotation is really Mendelssohn, although Elgar himself identified it.[64]

The Helen Weaver theory convincingly relates Op. 36 to Elgar's emotional life, yet it does not command universal acceptance.[65] Perhaps it may appear that Elgar's unbroken memory of an earlier love tarnishes his marriage. But although Elgar transferred to Alice an epithet already used for Helen ('Braut'), their relationship was different in kind. She was not an aspiring professional musician, and she was older than Elgar, a helpmeet whose love may have comprehended the maternal and accepted that their loves need not be equal: 'Thou giv'st me what thou canst, I give thee all.'[66] Elgar may have regarded their relation as complementary and intended to symbolise this in C.A.E. when he sketched the rhythm to reverse the palindrome of the theme (Ex. 5.2).

To suggest that such a relationship is sullied by Elgar regretting what he had lost is to take a naively romantic view of love and loyalty. Whether or not his regret was confessed on his deathbed to Newman, or admitted to Burley and, it seems, to Atkins, it may be that Helen's was the imagined soul, or one of them, enshrined in the violin concerto. There is no doubt that the dedicatee of XIII is Lady Mary Lygon.[67] But that XIII and the concerto could have both overt and concealed dedications (on top of the formal dedication of the concerto to Fritz Kreisler) is consistent with Elgar's way of thinking, as it was of Berg's.[68] The concealment practised by Elgar seems neither unlikely nor discreditable; and it would not surprise me to learn that Alice knew all about Helen Weaver.

Conclusion

If there is anything interesting to discover beyond the notes, it must be on the multivalent lines suggested first by the baffled Mrs Powell, and more recently in the divergent ideas of Sams, van Houten, Trowell, and Rollett. Reviewing these ideas, I am as much impressed by the persistence and intelligence of some solutions as by the ineptitude of others; yet only rarely do they suspend my scepticism. At the risk of dismissing something which may yet be unequivocally proven, I suggest that the 'right' solution, if it exists, while fulfilling the criteria, must be multivalent, must deal with musical as well as cryptographic issues, must produce workable counterpoint within Elgar's stylistic range, and must at the same time seem obvious (and not just to its begetter).

Some of the solutions offer insight into a fertile musical mind, yet none adds anything to comprehension of the actual sounds which constitute the work in performance.[69] And the standard of proof, even for well-considered commentaries, may always be too high given the maddeningly deficient quantity and quality of evidence, a situation which Elgar, under repeated questioning, may have decided was in his best interests. Multivalent solutions begin from Richard Powell's suggestion that the hidden theme might simultaneously embody a signifier and its signified: *Auld lang syne* and 'friendship' (but where is the 'dark saying'?). The Westrup–Parrott G.R.S.-based solution barks better than it bites, but Parrott's case for I Corinthians offers a fine saying, darker than *Religio Medici* although less suited to a piece involving the composer's friends. Sams produces thoughtful cryptic evidence, meeting all criteria except that the solution should seem obvious. This condition was smartly met by van Houten; but his musical evidence (the five notes of *Rule, Britannia* meet no authorised criterion) is weaker than the idea of an anagram on a five-finger exercise.[70] If his premises are accepted, Rollett (the most recent solution at the time of writing) meets all criteria other than the fifth (the falling sevenths). Unfortunately, his wide-ranging survey of previous solutions neglects the fascinating network of connections proposed by Trowell.[71]

Surveying so much of which its authors are convinced (and increasingly wary of titles including 'solution' or 'answer'), one must query to what extent any one solution rules out any other; unfortunately, few solvers trouble to refute other theories. Perhaps there is no need. The fact that the bass is from *Caractacus* does not contradict the tune's partial relation to the *Pathétique* sonata and the 'Prague', while using the 'never' notes of *Rule, Britannia* and fitting surprisingly well, among other tunes, with *Auld lang syne*. The only solutions which it may be safe to rule out are those based on false chronology; yet even here we cannot be perfectly certain that ideas for 'Nimrod' or G.R.S. (whether or not originally associated with those persons) were not already fermenting in Elgar's brain when, refreshed by a cigar (any clues there?), he sat down to improvise on Friday 21 October 1898.

6

Postscript

The tempo variations that arise in the course of an Elgar work are so subtle and elastic that they demand from the conductor and performer an almost complete infatuation with the music. For Elgar's music will not play by itself; merely to supervise it and give it progressional routine playing will only serve to immobilize it.

It may well be, in the *Enigma Variations*, that the problem is more readily understood by conductors of different nationality and musical background owing to the shortened musical form . . . (Bernard Herrmann)[1]

Variations in history: performance practice

The Musical Times, being somewhat *parti-pris*, acclaimed *Variations* after the first performance, perhaps operating a double standard: it dismissed Rimsky-Korsakov's suite *Snégourotchka* (*sic*) as 'an exercise in orchestration . . . but as music . . . beneath contempt', while in 'Dorabella' 'Berlioz himself need not have been ashamed of owning to this masterpiece of exquisitely refined scoring.' Jaeger himself, though he complained that the finale was too short, continued: 'Here is an English musician who has something to say and knows how to say it in his own individual and beautiful way . . . Effortless originality [is] combined with thorough *savoir faire*, and most important of all, beauty of theme . . .'[2]

These sentiments were entirely in line with the views of other critics, and Novello's selected the most favourable for a series of column-length advertisements in *The Musical Times*. Several epithets appear more than once, among them 'clever', 'ingenious' (also 'well-wrought'), and 'humorous'; aspects singled out more than once for praise are the contrasts within the set and the orchestration. The *Guardian* claimed Elgar as 'the most eminent master of orchestral effect which our country has produced, with the possible exception of Sir Arthur Sullivan'. The *Morning Post* and *Daily Graphic* both commended the revised coda, as had *The Musical Times* itself in November; the *Daily News* (confirmed by the *Daily Chronicle*) reported that ' "Nimrod" and "Dorabella" were much applauded', an expression of enthusiasm which, interrupting the sequence of variations, would be frowned upon today.[3] Time has not overturned the verdict of the earliest critics, and has shown that the Englishness of *Variations*, as the composer of the music to *Psycho* implied (see epigraph), is no obstacle to interpretation and appreciation by foreign conductors or audiences.

Variations established Elgar as an international figure when it was conducted by Julius Buths in Düsseldorf on 7 February 1901, some months before his celebrated redemption of the initial failure of *The Dream of Gerontius*. Alexander Siloti directed the successful Russian premiere in 1904. In the years before the First World War broke out in 1914, the international *réclame* of *Variations* may be measured by the distinguished conductors who performed it, including Weingartner, Nikisch, Mahler, and Beecham. Henry Wood conducted it as early as 1901, and recorded it twice (1925 and 1936). Between the world wars, leading Elgar conductors working in Britain included Harty and Boult, both of whom made early recordings (1932 and 1936). Others, including Toscanini and Monteux, made recordings after 1950, as did Beecham ('one of the most fascinating there is').[4] Barbirolli, who first recorded the work in 1947, was bracketed with Toscanini (whose live 1935 performance survives) by insular criticism of excessive emotionalism, but in his recordings the fluctuations of tempo (surely an index of emotionalism) are considerably less than the composer's own.

Developments in performance practice during the twentieth century affect not only tempo but articulation and style more generally, although they may matter less than the preferences and temperament of the conductor: even balletic 'Dorabella' can vary between the gymnasium (Ormandy, taking a lead from Toscanini's muscular viola solo) and the crepuscular (Boult). Regrettably, Richter's performances have left no quantifiable trace in the form of recordings or detailed criticism. But when recordings eventually appeared, the performance trends were partly set by Elgar himself, the first composer to record a truly representative selection of his own compositions. In his 1926 recording of

Variations, Elgar did not adhere slavishly to markings in his own score. Having slowed several variations before publication, including II, VIII, and 'Nimrod', he now drastically slows the theme itself to Adagio ($\downarrow = c$. 44 at first, well below the marked 63). This move has been widely imitated by passionately romantic Elgarians such as Solti, and more dispassionate ones like Beecham; it is normal, in fact, to hear the theme beginning in the region 40–48. Classic Elgarians like Boult and, for so he now appears, Barbirolli (1955), work towards a moderate Andante, $\downarrow = 56$; these conductors tend to restore something near their theme tempo for R.P.A., which it is normal to hear faster than the theme, but slower than the metronome mark.[5] The tempo of C.A.E. follows from interpretation of the theme, but its texture demands a steadier pulse, often that of the B section of the theme. The custom is well established of taking the theme's B section with greater regularity and flow, and slowing down again for A'. This can apply to other sections, notably 'Nimrod' and R.P.A.; in the latter, Elgar slightly increases speed with the rapid passage-work of the laughing B section.

Steadier tempi are certainly not the result of age or lassitude on the part of the sixty-nine-year-old composer. Although setting off well below the metronomic speed ($\downarrow = 40$), 'Nimrod' is by no means overindulged, nor is it a dirge; Elgar adds an unmarked *stringendo* (cue 34) to counterbalance the first, and precede the second, *largamente* (36:3, 36:11), reaching $\downarrow = c$. 56, a little above his metronome mark. The final very sudden diminuendo is managed with less ritardando than is usual, creating a rapid deflation rather than milking the harmonically simple cadence for tears. Most conductors accept Elgar's implied revision, starting 'Nimrod' in the range $\downarrow = 40$–44 (Boult is even slower), and some maintain it throughout. From a virtually standing start, Solti also reaches $\downarrow = c$. 56, but his acceleration is married to a crescendo, equating speed with volume; not flexibility but mere tautology.

Elgar whips such virtuoso pieces as 'Troyte' and G.R.S. fully up to speed, and dances through 'Dorabella' 'a leetle' faster than most. H.D.S-P. is faster than the printed marking ($\downarrow. = 72$), although less than the 84 in the sketch; Elgar's $\downarrow. = c$. 80 is followed by several conductors, and he also provides justification for a tendency, deplored by 'Dorabella', to take W.M.B. faster than marked.[6] For W.N., Elgar's tempo is widely accepted, whereas for 'Nimrod' the identical quaver value is seldom

Ex. 6.1 *Portamenti* in Elgar's 1926 recording of 'Nimrod'

maintained (see p. 61). But variations of medium pulse, including R.B.T. and all the female portraits after C.A.E., are unaffected by the tendency, started by the composer, towards more extreme tempi. The chief objective of this tendency seems to be to accentuate contrasts to an extent not envisaged at the time of publication.

The slowing of the theme may reflect Elgar's view of it through the dark glass of time: triumphs and failures, desolate streams (*The Music Makers*), and the death of Alice. Every other contrast and articulation receives devoted attention in his superb performance. The effect is only a little diminished by doubling the bass line throughout with a tuba, incapable of *portamento* (never mind pizzicato: the end of 'Ysobel' touches the grotesque). This counter to the technical difficulty of recording low frequencies is not the only element which alters the balance implied in the score; Elgar surely brought out on purpose the thematic trumpet rhythm under the C.A.E. quotation in the finale (73:7) despite its being marked pianissimo.

From this cursory review of tempi in performances of *Variations*, it may follow that authentic stylistic features, such as tempi, need not be imitated, but may legitimately conform to the tastes and practices of the period of performance, and to the acoustics of individual halls. Until recently, at least, modern audiences might not have accepted the swift *portamento*, amounting to glissando, in bars 7 and 8 of the theme (the fourth beats, the slide in part a response to the tenuto: see Ex. 2.1), or heard the 'good loveable honest SOUL' of Jaeger in the delicately swooning start of 'Nimrod' – still less the 'inauthentic' war memorial.[7] In Ex. 6.1, first violin *portamenti* are shown with a line rather than a slur. *Portamenti* occur in other parts, and continue throughout: in 34:5 the violins play the falling major seventh (the only difference from 33:5) *portamento* although there is no slur in the score; the same happens with the quavers in 36:2–3, and this is far from an exhaustive catalogue. In the theme, Kennedy counts eighteen slides, a figure confirmed by Robert Philip in a comparative table.[8]

Like other recordings with composers at the helm, Elgar's will necessarily give pause both to those whose concept of rightness is based on the score, and to those who locate it in a composer's recordings; both are authoritative, even when they disagree. Nevertheless, as Robert Philip puts it, they have a unique ring of authenticity

> not just in the limited sense that they reproduce what he did. They are also authentic in a deeper sense: they show a composer working with musicians whose style and habits, abilities and limitations, were an integral part of his own musical world. They are authentic because, quite simply, they are the real thing.[9]

Philip provides evidence that Elgar implicitly accepted changing orchestral styles through his performing career, including different handling of, for instance, *portamento* and vibrato; new styles may have encouraged freshness in readings of his work. Elgar might object to a musical performance sounding uninvolved or dry and (like Ormandy) eschewing the rhythmic freedom he himself enjoyed; but he might not in principle object to the orchestral sound, with metal strings, wider-bored brass, and timpani skins of man-made fibre, which we normally hear today, nor to our perpetual string vibrato and absence of *portamento* (unless specified). No harm is done, however, by recognising that things have changed. Perhaps the movement towards restoration of contemporary performance practice, which has already advanced well into the twentieth century, will habituate us to the seductions of a 'true' Elgarian style, with the convincing evidence, not available with earlier composers, of his own example.

Later recordings of *Variations* are so numerous that a reasoned discography is beyond the scope of this volume; it has been recorded with apparent relish by orchestras and conductors world-wide. If I had to choose one for a desert island, and if Elgar's recording were not allowed, it would either be Barbirolli for his well-moderated assurance, which allows the music without exaggeration to be both pretty and emotional;

or for musicality and daring, in an approach no more 'English' than many an American or Hungarian, it would be Beecham for his noble rubato in 'Nimrod', quite differently paced from Elgar's, his elegant (slow) 'Dorabella', his brass, rasping yet superbly controlled, his glittering triangle. There is no better testimony than such a performance to the truth that *Variations*, in Elgar's words, 'should stand simply as a "piece" of music'.

And finally

The enigma: what of it? If anything may be said firmly, it is:

(1) If the enigma is encoded in musical sound, it can only be an unconsummated symbol, open to diverse interpretations.

(2) Elgar did not use the word, so far as we know, until May 1899 and it was added over the third bar of the MS score by Jaeger, aiming at central placement on the first page of the published score (where it remains). There is nothing – unless after all it concerns the identities of the 'friends' – to suggest it played any role in the conception and composition of *Variations*.[10]

(3) The theme, increasingly melancholy as its tempo became slower, may represent Elgar as he saw himself; a lonely and misunderstood artist, frustrated in his ambition towards major symphonic composition. This metaphorical signification appears beyond reasonable doubt, and for better reasons than the mere possibility of singing the composer's name to the first four notes and reversing them in bar 2: as Geoffrey Poole suggests, 'Elgar, Edward', 'in the questioning sense of "Who He?"' Herrmann 'always felt that the enigma of the *Variations* was not a musical one, but rather a personal attitude . . . the enigma of the composer himself'. Reed confirmed 'he was himself the enigma'.[11]

(4) If the enigma is the A section, its character is affected by closure on a major chord; Elgar proudly labelled the *tierce de Picardie* in the sketch and it adumbrates a series of minor–major steps throughout the composition. The first (bar 7) lightens the atmosphere and merges A into the flow, elegance, and warmth of the B section.

(5) The continuity of C.A.E. from the theme and its reappearance with 'Nimrod' in the finale recognise the exceptional support given him

by two people (if there is a quotation of the enigmatic (***) it is, perhaps significantly, not literal). The finale represents Elgar himself, in a promising burst of symphonism, and originally it ended dismissively, as if to say 'take it or leave it'; the revised ending is 'take it or it will be the worse for you', a thoroughly original version of the apotheosis-coda beloved of the nineteenth century.

(6) The intervening variations allegedly portray people and incidents we can only know at second hand.[12] Elgar warns that some variations have only a tenuous connection with the theme. Also, although he does not warn us, his descriptions of the models sometimes relate only tenuously to the music; indeed, the evidence adduced here may suggest that even if music is capable of portraiture, most of the variations are not in reality portraits at all. From this we may infer a higher objective, to display to the audience a gallery of musical characterisations, and one can see why it appealed to Holst whose *The Planets* was also an orchestral epiphany for a composer over forty.[13] If we grasp the characterisations, neither programmatically nor abstractly but musically, we need not be concerned with initials and nicknames. Even with XIII, despite its elliptical thematic handling and intertextuality (Mendelssohn), who or what inspired it counts for less than its intrinsic properties, as a strained vision of ideal and loss, a cold dawn before the brilliant sunrise of the finale. *Mutatis mutandis*, the same applies to every variation and intermezzo.

But the enigma? *Variations* is both public, in its broader musical gestures and its strongly marked characterisations, and private, in its internal cross-references and its gallery of portraits. Since the enigma was not solved by revealing the identities of the 'friends', it is tempting to read it as a public statement, an idea preached, as it were, to the unsuspecting audience. Abstractions cannot be tested like counterpoint, but an impressive body of opinion proposes the 'larger theme' of friendship. Even if, late in 1898, Elgar felt betrayed by his friends, the spiritual dimension of *Religio Medici*'s definition of friendship makes an appealing verbal metaphor for what the music may be doing. One alternative larger theme, patriotism, sits uneasily with the nature of the composition; Elgar having thumped a patriotic tub in the Diamond Jubilee cantata *The Banner of St George*, and perhaps with more conviction in *Caractacus*, wrote *Variations* partly because he felt unable to get to grips with a symphony on a patriotic theme. Had he been able to write 'Gordon', the variations might never have existed. If not friendship, celebration of art represents a better understanding of the music than imperial triumphalism.

Regrettably, most enigma 'solutions' resolve nothing. To find sources in Elgar's earlier music or in music by others is merely to say that Elgar composed music in the ordinary way, in the light of earlier music; that is no enigma. Looking for a source for the melody is to ignore the composer's hints; and none of the proposed counterpoints has the *Klang* of inevitability. Even if *Auld lang syne* were the least bad fit, the number of different manipulations with which it can be made nearly convincing weakens the case; and the more different tunes that are proposed, the less likely the case becomes for any one of them. Recent research on ciphers reflects a postmodern mingling of scientific positivism (a cipher ought to be 'right' or, of course, wrong) with fantasy. Unfortunately, criteria for evaluation of ciphers seem no less arbitrary than for counterpoints. Against ciphers, too, is the inherent probability that Elgar invented music by the process we normally call inspiration: 'My idea is that there is music in the air . . . you – simply – simply – take as much as you require!'[14] What you take, he might have added, you manipulate to satisfy yourself aesthetically. It seems unlikely that he arrived at a theme so austerely simple, internally complex, and exquisitely balanced, by means of games with letters. And if a cipher, however ingenious, does not reveal something of Elgar's compositional thinking, what is it for?

Just as the variations are caprices more or less tenuously related to the structure of the theme, so Elgar's clues about the enigma may have only tenuous connections with the creative process which led to the composition of *Variations*. The three significant uses of the theme (A, including its 'Nimrod' formulation) in *The Music Makers* already belong to the interpretative history of the earlier work; they may reveal more about Elgar in 1912 than about Elgar in 1898. By 1918, after the chilly reception of his Second Symphony and the equivocal response to *Falstaff*, and with war still raging, Elgar's reminiscence of the third bar with its aching seventh at a late climax in his Violin Sonata is the more touching for its relative concealment and the lack of motivation by mere words. He may have added this detail after hearing of the death of the intended dedicatee, Marie Joshua, but like the whole Cello Concerto (1919) it may also be heard as an ardent gesture of resignation: his own sun was setting.[15] These reminiscences, however, do confirm that Elgar associated the theme with artistic loneliness.

Those commentators are therefore probably correct who have seen in *Variations* a metaphor for the artist combating the depression, neglect, and discouragement which he felt was his lot, and planning to take the public by storm (or offering marvels if only people would listen). This, too, is hardly an enigma; the passage from minor to major, from metaphorical strife to triumph, *per ardua ad astra*, is common in nineteenth-century composition, even without a programme. Beethoven's Fifth Symphony is the obvious paradigm, followed by Brahms's First, Bruckner's Eighth, and so forth; Elgar's originality lies in compressing a symphonic archetype into a theme and variations, lasting under half an hour.

But the enigma? Among the seductive explanations, none seems quite to cover the necessary conditions in a consistent and convincing fashion. The search is not helped by secrecy, inconsistency, and perhaps disingenuousness in Elgar's own comments, and those of other people who may have been in a position to know something. If the dead could send postcards, solvers would all get one saying 'it won't do'. In saluting those who have laboured long at this curiously fascinating, if unrewarding, problem, I remain agnostic in the matter: where Elgar's creative intention is concerned, I am by no means sure that there is anything to solve. Perhaps if he could have foreseen the consequences Elgar might have suppressed his urge thus to catch the public ear by mystification. Solutions have become part of musical history and of the reception history of Op. 36. But if we attend to the music it will unfold its own story, having little need of insights from those who have grappled (and will continue to grapple) with what Elgar, as the musically trained French playwright Eric-Emmanuel Schmitt insists, took with him to the grave: 'the beauty of a mystery, after all, resides in the secret that inhabits it, and not in the truth that it conceals'.[16]

Eric Sams describes the finale 'as an allegory of renaissance, with strong overtones of ringing out the old and ringing in the new'; he compares the throbbing bass, below the greeting whistle which ushers in the return of C.A.E., as 'a midnight of minims'.[17] It may be worth recalling that Op. 36 was begun as a winter of discontent came on apace and Birchwood seemed 'damp and rheumaticky', and was completed in February, when the season of natural revival was imminent. Within that year, 1899, Elgar buried the provincial 'Malvern composer'; by means of intimate portraits, mainly of his Malvern circle, *Variations* heralded the glorious twenty-year summer of Britain's first international master of symphonic music.

Appendix

Melodies 'fitted' to Elgar's theme

The appendix takes the form of an exercise in counterpoint, using Elgar's theme in lieu of the traditional cantus firmus; hence no phrasing is indicated. The other melodies are not meant to fit with each other, but only with the theme.

Contrapuntal faults are indicated as follows:

/   virtual identity over several notes (a virtue for a 'source' melody)
5   a perfect fifth approached by similar or parallel motion, and thus poor or wrong as counterpoint
4   an exposed fourth, which may be rectified by appropriate bass-notes
X   simply does not fit

(a)   App. 1: 'Enigma' in the major mode, such as often occurs, although not with the original rhythmic values given here.

The second and third lines are not counterpoints but melodies proposed as a source:

1   Beethoven: *Pathétique* sonata Op. 13; fits the theme as well as the 'Nimrod' version which is said to be derived from it. Double note-values, transposed from A♭

2   Mozart: 'Prague' Symphony K. 504; showing relation to sections A and B of the theme, but only with an interruption

The remainder test whether these themes 'go' with Elgar's:

3   Elgar: *The Light of Life*, 'Meditation', halved note-values. After a blatant consecutive, a good start; severe problems from bar 3

4   *Auld lang syne*; severe problems in bars 3–4. The échappé in bar 1 is unfortunate in counterpoint. The tempo of the theme is quite wrong

for this melody. The resemblance resumes after a gap in bars 5–6, as suggested by Richard Powell; his *Auld lang syne*, partly in G minor, is contrapuntally no different from this version

5 *Loch Lomond* can be accommodated by a good bass (at marked fourths); both tunes can be played at something like their proper tempo

6 The National Anthem; rests must be omitted from the theme. Bars 4–5 require careful handling but something might be made of it

(b) App. 2: 'Enigma' in the minor mode.

1 *Auld lang syne* in B♭ major; brings some trouble towards the end

2 *Home, Sweet Home* in B♭ major, but it cannot accommodate the change of mode. Good for four bars, better than if it were in G where, however, it might be considered more a source than a counterpoint

3 Brahms: Symphony No. 4, halved note-values, transposed from E minor (compare Ex. 2.2: I have omitted the first note). After the unison in bar 1, some pretty dovetailing; a doubtful bar 4 and fails in bar 5

It is hard to see reasons for preferring one of these counterpoints to another on musical grounds, and even if they fitted the bass of the theme, none, I believe, would have been good enough for Elgar.

Appendix: examples of counterpoints to the theme
App. 1 Theme in G major

App. 1 Theme in G major (*cont.*)

App. 2 Theme in G minor

Enigma

Auld lang syne

Home, sweet home

Brahms
Symphony No. 4

Notes

Introduction

1 From lecture notes 'England and her Music', in Ralph Vaughan Williams and Gustav Holst, *Heirs and Rebels*, edited by Ursula Vaughan Williams and Imogen Holst. London: Oxford University Press, 1959, p. 50.

2 *Elgar Complete Edition* XXVII (London and Sevenoaks: Novello, 1986), hereafter cited as *Complete Edition*.

3 The MS is in the British Library (Add. MS 58004); several pages are used to illustrate Elgar, *My Friends Pictured Within* (hereafter *MFPW*).

4 Illustrated in *MFPW* and Eulenburg Miniature Score 884.

5 Moore, *Elgar and his Publishers: Letters of a Creative Life* (hereafter *Publishers*), p. 128; cited p. 16.

6 See the full and miniature scores (including those published by Eulenburg) and *Complete Edition*.

7 The introduction (pp. v–xi) is jointly signed by Robert Anderson and Jerrold Northrop Moore; the critical notes (pp. xvi–xxiv) are signed by Robert Anderson.

8 Richter added '*and not only in this country*'. Reported by Reed, *Elgar*, p. 97. See also Fifield, *True Artist and True Friend*, p. 411.

9 Shera, *Elgar: Instrumental Works* I, p. 11.

10 Constant Lambert, *Music Ho!* (London: Faber and Faber, 1934), p. 240.

11 The 'classic' recording by Sargent, April 1945; see Michael Kennedy, 'Some Elgar Interpreters', in Monk (ed.), *Elgar Studies*, p. 233, and John Knowles, 'A Select Elgar Discography', ibid., p. 248.

1 Composition

1 Moore, *Edward Elgar: A Creative Life* (hereafter *Creative Life*), p. 217; Parry, *Summary of Musical History* (1904), cited by Michael Pope, '*King Olaf* and the English Choral Tradition', in Monk (ed.), *Elgar Studies*, p. 56.

2 Kennedy, *Portrait of Elgar* (hereafter *Portrait*), p. 28. All references are to the third edition.

3 Moore, *Edward Elgar: Letters of a Lifetime* (hereafter *Letters of a Lifetime*), p. 56. Moore, *Creative Life*, p. 229 and Anderson, *Elgar*, pp. 36–7 name portraits of St Augustine and Caractacus, but it is clear that the Augustine project would have been a cantata.

4 Moore speculates that some may have gone into *Caractacus*: *Creative Life*, p. 230.

5 On the chronology of the *Gordon* project and the Worcestershire Philharmonic, see Moore, *Creative Life*, p. 246, quoting a theme later used in *Gerontius* (e.g. Prelude fig. 12); Anderson, *Elgar*, pp. 37–9.

6 *Enigma Variations*, Royal Ballet 1966; see David Vaughan, *Frederick Ashton and his Ballets* (London: Adam and Charles Black, 1977), pp. 356–63. This was not the first ballet to use the music, but Frank Staff's, presented in wartime by the Ballet Rambert and London Ballet, was abstract.

7 'Jäger [Jaeger]' is German for 'hunter'. See *Genesis* X: 9.

8 It may be of interest that three female portraits, Ysobel, W.N., and (***), make use of the melodic échappé, where the third degree of the scale skips to the tonic without the intervening second (e.g. 19:4; 32:8; 55:5). This shape is not otherwise prominent in *Variations*.

9 Mrs Richard Powell (née Dora Penny), *Edward Elgar: Memories of a Variation* (hereafter *Memories*).

10 Young goes through the Worcestershire friends impartially: *Elgar O.M.*, pp. 83–5, and 'Friends Pictured Within', in Monk (ed.), *Elgar Studies*, pp. 81–106 (hereafter 'Friends'). See also Reed, *Elgar*, pp. 46–7 and 52–3, and the personalia in Anderson, *Elgar*, pp. 455–65.

11 Elgar's letter to Novello's of 17 November 1898 concerns payment to Acworth: Moore, *Publishers*, pp. 97–8. The librettist of *The Light of Life*, Edward Capel-Cure, who later married a sister of 'Ysobel', was also excluded: Young, 'Friends', p. 93.

12 See Atkins, *The Elgar–Atkins Friendship*, p. 38, where, however, I.A. is incorrectly said to have been overlaid with G.R.S. in the sketch (see p. 15). Atkins wrote a pedagogical introduction to *Variations* in *The Musical Times* 75 (1934), pp. 328–30 and 411–14, without mentioning his own exclusion or purporting to 'solve the enigma'.

13 Burley's memories were published posthumously with a co-author (Frank C. Carruthers) as *Edward Elgar: The Record of a Friendship* (hereafter Burley); see pp. 115, 120.

14 Burley, p. 115. Alice's diary confirms that they left Leeds on 8 October (my thanks to Brian Trowell for this information), as predicted by Elgar (to Jaeger: 'If you want me I shall be at the Queen's Hotel Leeds till Saturday', i.e. 8 October): Moore, *Publishers*, p. 92. On the *Caractacus* premiere, see Moore, *Creative Life*, pp. 243–5; Maine, *Elgar* I, pp. 77–82.

15 Elgar met him in 1882 and they communicated until Buck's death in 1932. Buck was among the few who attended the Elgars' wedding (Kennedy, *Portrait*, p. 43); see also W. R. Mitchell, *Mr Elgar and Dr Buck: A Musical Friendship* (Giggleswick: Castleberg, 1991).

16 Anderson, *Elgar*, p. 318; Young, 'Friends', pp. 88–93.

17 Moore, *Letters of a Lifetime*, p. 70. Kilburn's letter is dated 20 November; Elgar's reply (as late as 6 January 1899) mentions 'I have completed nearly a set of Variations for orchestra which *I* like – but commercially nothing', ibid., p. 73.

18 Burley (p. 126) says Parry and Sullivan variations were 'discarded', suggesting they may have been improvised in her presence. Maine quotes Elgar as saying that they had been abandoned 'as the suggestion of their musical styles seemed more obvious than the allusions to unmusical things in the rest of the work, and in another mode from them': *Elgar* II, p. 101.

19 Powell, *Memories*, p. 100.

20 This account is conflated from Elgar, *MFPW*, which indicates the inspiration behind individual variations; the narrative in J. A. Forsyth, 'Edward Elgar: True Artist and True Friend', in *The Music Student* 12 (December 1932), p. 243, quoted in *Complete Edition*, pp. v–viii, and excerpted in Moore, *Creative Life*, pp. 247–50; and accounts in Powell, *Memories*, pp. 12–13; Burley, pp. 116–29; Kennedy, *Portrait*, pp. 77–82; Moore, *Creative Life*, pp. 247–56; Anderson, *Elgar*, pp. 39–41.

21 Cited from Maine, *Elgar* II, p. 101, as 'the words of Elgar himself'. For Moore the word 'nothing' implies creative uncertainty (*Creative Life*, p. 249), but what Elgar said might apply to the openings of many significant compositions, such as Beethoven's *Eroica*.

22 As worded in Forsyth; Maine has the same story in different words.

23 See, for instance, Reed, *Elgar as I Knew Him*, pp. 23ff. On Elgar's early talent in improvisation see Kennedy, *Portrait*, pp. 19–20. The piano in question was the instrument at Forli, in Malvern, not the square piano installed at Birchwood, the nearby cottage which Elgar rented for prolonged work on his scores. Perhaps because it was winter, very little work on *Variations* seems to have been done at Birchwood, other than the revision of the finale.

24 Letter of 20 October 1898: Moore, *Publishers*, p. 93.

25 Ibid., p. 94.

26 Ibid., pp. 95–6, 100, 102.

27 British Library, Add. MS 58003. Details of sketches are in *Complete Edition*, pp. xvi–xviii.

28 Burley, p. 116. Sketches, fo. 6, on music paper; transcribed *Complete Edition*, p. xvi. Other lists apparently concern the ordering of the variations once completed; see chapter 4.

29 See Brian Trowell, 'Elgar's Use of Literature' (hereafter 'Literature'), in Monk (ed.), *Edward Elgar: Music and Literature*, pp. 309–10 (note 169).

30 Powell, *Memories*, p. 12. Her memory, of course, may have been faulty.

31 The original ending (facsimile, *Complete Edition*, p. xii) is signed and dated 'Feb. 18 1898 [*sic*] Malvern (Forli)'.

32 Letter to Jaeger, 13 March 1899: Moore, *Publishers*, p. 114.

33 Fifield, *True Artist and True Friend*, pp. 309–10; Dibble, *C. Hubert H. Parry*, pp. 368–9.

34 *The Musical Times* 40 (July 1899): profile pp. 441–7, review pp. 464, 471.

35 Moore, *Publishers*, pp. 128–9. The page reference is to the piano version. Richter's full agreement that there should be a revision is confirmed in Atkins, *The Elgar–Atkins Friendship*, p. 40.

36 The page (facsimile, *Complete Edition*, p. xiii) is signed 'Edward Elgar Birchwood Lodge'. The words are from Longfellow, *Elegiac Verse*; as Brian Trowell notes, Elgar probably meant the citation ironically, for Longfellow continues: 'Many a poem is marred by a superfluous verse' ('Literature', p. 216).

37 Kennedy, *Portrait*, pp. 88–90; Moore, *Creative Life*, pp. 285, 289, 292.

38 See Anderson, *Elgar*, p. 41; Moore, *Letters of a Lifetime*, p. 78.

39 S. Banfield, 'England, 1918–45', in Robert P. Morgan (ed.), *Man and Music: Modern Times: From World War I to the Present* (London: Macmillan, 1993), pp. 183–4.

2 Variations: the theme

1 I am indebted to Jeremy Dibble for lending me his unpublished paper 'Fantasy and Hybridisation in the British Variation Tradition'.

2 Dibble notes that, like Elgar's, Parry's *Variations* had international success: *C. Hubert H. Parry*, pp. 342–5.

3 In view of theories concerning a popular melody and the 'enigma' (see chapter 6), it is noteworthy that the themes are often not English, but include Irish, African, and American melodies. Hurlstone had written *Variations on an Original Theme* in 1896; his *Variations on a Hungarian Air* followed in 1899, and his *Fantasie-Variations on a Swedish Air* in 1904, the year of Delius's *Appalachia*.

4 Elgar and Bantock follow Strauss (*Ein Heldenleben*, 1897–8) in depicting their wives musically, but precede Mahler (Sixth Symphony).

5 Kennedy mentions *Carnaval*: *Portrait*, p. 81. Shera suggests that variation II is related in technique to the first of Schumann's *Etudes symphoniques*: *Elgar: Instrumental Works* I, p. 20.

6 The comparison with *Don Quixote* was made as early as 1904 by Alfred Kalisch, who contrasted the works' objectives: Strauss shows 'one character or type modified by, yet persisting through, every change of circumstance'. See Young, 'Friends', in Monk (ed.), *Elgar Studies*, p. 84. Diana McVeagh points out that unlike Strauss Elgar 'keeps the caesura between variations': *Edward Elgar*, p. 160.

7 Each pair of bars forms, in Messiaen's term, a nonretrogradable rhythm, the same read backwards as forwards, a point Elgar noted much later (see *Complete Edition*, p. vi). The theme forms an illustration of Seeger's logical division of music into 'moods': see Raymond Monelle, *Linguistics and Semiotics in Music* (Chur: Harwood Academic Publishers, 1992), pp. 76–80.

8 Reed suggested something like a template, but as a precompositional stage of the melody itself, not for the variations: *Elgar*, p. 153.

9 Brahms's theme, transposed and in halved note-values, fits Elgar's as a counterpoint for four bars, better than some tunes which have been offered as 'solutions' to the enigma (see chapter 5 and appendix).

3 Friends pictured within

1 Specific page references are not given. See Newman, *Elgar*, pp. 137–49; Tovey, *Essays in Musical Analysis* IV, pp. 149–52; Elgar, *MFPW*, no pagination; Powell, *Memories*, pp. 101–17; Burley, pp. 121–7; Young, 'Friends', in Monk (ed.), *Elgar Studies*, pp. 81–106.

2 *Die Zauberflöte*, no. 7: Man and wife, and wife and man aspire to the level of gods.

3 Kennedy, *Elgar Orchestral Music*, p. 23; Reed, *Elgar*, p. 154.

4 The score appears confusing because the violins are written in G♭ / D♭; the sensitive note of the modulation is the bass, which descends through B♮ and rises through B♯.

5 However, not knowing the subject, Johnstone in the *Guardian* (9 February 1900, presumably after Richter's Manchester performance) rained epithets on R.B.T. including 'garrulous,' 'querulous', and 'ape-like' (Kennedy, *Portrait*, p. 91).

6 IV was among the earliest variations conceived, perhaps against the 6–8–6 phrasing of the theme which Elgar seems to have contemplated.

7 Young, 'Friends', p. 96; *Alice Elgar: Enigma of a Victorian Lady* (London: Dennis Dobson, 1978), pp. 43–4.

8 It is more than likely that some sketches are lost, but R.P.A. appears without musical notation, though with pencilled key and metre, in the list

of incipits on sketch fo. 6; fo. 19v contains a short score, unique in this collection of sketches, of the upper wind and horns for 17:1–7, without the bass melody.

9 Note the use of timpani in octaves (G–g, which is exceptionally high) with an intervening C.

10 Maine also invokes healthy exercise: *Elgar* I, p. 68.

11 ♩.=52 and this supplementary direction are reproduced in *Complete Edition*. The first printed editions had ♩=52, which is odd in 6/8 but corresponds to Elgar's own recorded tempo; see footnote in the Eulenburg score, p. 47, and Del Mar, *Conducting Elgar*, p. 10

12 Moore, *Creative Life*, p. 241. One of Elgar's most touching late letters is to Florence Norbury: Moore, *Letters of a Lifetime*, p. 473. Frivolity (reproved by her sister) is a characteristic of the original Dorabella, in *Così fan tutte*.

13 Irregular because diatonic: the top notes of the sevenths are E♭–D (semitone), then G–F (tone): in B♭ major, degrees 4–3 and 6–5. The harmony differs correspondingly.

14 13 March 1899: Moore, *Publishers*, p. 115.

15 Kennedy analyses the confusion of dates, probably the result of time telescoped in Elgar's memory, by which some part, at least, of what Elgar recalled happened after the composition of 'Nimrod': *Portrait*, pp. 92–3.

16 The Referendum Party, which made much noise but little impact in the 1997 British parliamentary election, used 'Nimrod' 'accompanied by evocative images such as cricket on the village green' on their campaign video, apparently 'unaware that the music was written to represent a German . . .': Geoffrey Hodgkins, 'From the Editor', *Elgar Society News* 2 (July 1997), p. 3. Yet the anti-European party was only responding to (and developing) the historical reception of the piece.

17 See Moore, *Creative Life*, p. 254; Reed, *Elgar as I Knew Him*, pp. 36–8.

18 This version should appease those who question the story on the grounds that bulldogs do not like water. That Dan enjoyed swimming is, however, confirmed by Percy Hull, who was photographed in 1896 with Sinclair, Elgar, and Dan in the organist's garden (Powell, *Memories*, pp. 112–13).

19 See Young, *Elgar O.M.*, appendix on pp. 398–401.

20 Reed, *Elgar*, p. 155.

21 See also Young, *Elgar O.M.*, p. 79; 'Friends', pp. 89–91.

22 In a close reading of this variation, Brian Trowell calls this a Neapolitan sixth, which is accurate with respect to the overall tonality, but not to the way the chord is reached and quitted: 'Literature', p. 223.

23 The chord begins in first inversion (the bass C below the cello A♭), moves to C minor for a bar, and is in root position only for 57:1–2. At cue 60 the E♭ chord is also in first inversion. The right effect is obtained if the timpani are played with a couple of heavy coins. At cue 58, Elgar leaves no time to change to normal sticks; Kennedy notes this as a rare miscalculation (*Portrait*, p. 97), but Del Mar points out that with coins rather than hard sticks the change is possible (*Conducting Elgar*, p. 18).

24 Shera, *Elgar Instrumental Works* I, p. 27.

25 On a sketch including a pattern of falling fourths, probably an early version of XIII, see Trowell, 'Literature', p. 220; but there is no evident relation to the theme of *Variations*.

26 *Complete Edition*, p. xix; Trowell, 'Literature', p. 219.

27 Moore, *Publishers*, p. 122.

28 Atkins in *The Musical Times* 75 (1934), p. 413.

29 Burley, p. 126. See also Young, *Elgar O.M.*, p. 87; Moore, *Creative Life*, pp. 263–4. Writing in 1931, Shera (*Elgar Instrumental Works* I, p. 27) states correctly that the dedicatee was 'about to embark on a sea voyage'. She returned after a few years and married (becoming Lady Mary Trefusis), removing her organisational energies to Cornwall (Young, 'Friends', p. 93).

30 Ernest Newman, 'Elgar and his Variations: What was the Enigma?', *Sunday Times*, 16, 23 and 30 April and 7 May 1939; quoted from Newman in the *Sunday Times*, 18 November 1956, cited in Kennedy, *Portrait*, p. 96.

4 A form of self-portraiture

1 Trowell, 'Literature', p. 312, notes that the bass of the theme derived from a fugue subject in *Caractacus*. Westrup suggests that the theme itself has the character of a countersubject, because of the 'missing' first beats: 'Elgar's Enigma', p. 84.

2 G, B minor, C, then by falling fifths, E minor, A minor, D, and back to G.

3 Moore associates this falling three-note figure with the Mendelssohn quotation in XIII (*Creative Life*, p. 265; see also Trowell, 'Literature', p. 221). The sketches (fo. 30v) show that Elgar may have planned an overt reprise of XIII: a note reads 'introduce L.M.L.'

4 Eric Sams, 'Variations on an Original Theme (Enigma)', p. 261.

5 Moore (*Creative Life*, p. 265) calls this 'the E.D.U. solution' to the enigma, but it is clearly 'Nimrod'.

6 See for instance the first finale to *Così fan tutte*: the last section has a seventy-bar cut authorised by Mozart, and its concentration on the tonic, like Elgar's, is enlivened by sallies into related keys.

7 On *Gerontius* see Moore, *Publishers*, pp. 200–9.

8 British Library Add. MS 499743B, catalogued as sketches 'made during piano solo arrangement' and bound with sketches for other works: see fos. 19–20. In the sketches, the main motive (E) appears with a simpler rhythm than in the orchestral score. Elgar was trying to complete the piano reduction before scoring the music, as was his normal practice. In this sketch, some passages are neatly written in ink, and are clearly piano music (with pedal marks); pianistically unplayable additions are made in pencil (marking, for instance, the bass at 78, while the left hand plays theme A).

9 The new ending has its critics, including Kennedy (*Portrait*, p. 98); Tovey called it 'tub-thumping' with its 'facile descent into *prestissimo* semibreves': 'Elgar, Master of Music', *Music and Letters* 16 (1935), p. 4. The Ashton ballet used the original ending: David Vaughan, *Frederick Ashton and his Ballets*, (London: Adam and Charles Black, 1977), p. 362. On the organ part, see Rainer Fanselau, *Die Orgel im Werk Edward Elgars* (*Göttinger Musikwissenschaftliche Arbeiten* 5, Göttingen: Andreas Funke, 1973), pp. 283, 286–8, 290–3.

10 Moore, *Letters of a Lifetime*, p. 205. Elgar claimed not to have noticed the thematic resemblance until it was pointed out by Reed: *Elgar*, p. 157.

11 Trowell, 'Literature', p. 222.

12 The list on which table 4.2, column 2, is based is crossed out; it is possibly in Alice's hand. The initials cueing columns 4 and 5 are those of the score, including ***, except that 'Ysobel' appears as I.F., but the order of this column corresponds to no other ordering (these lists are transcribed in *Complete Edition*, p. xvi).

13 On VIII–IX, see Powell, *Memories*, p. 109. The B.G.N. sketch in the Elgar Birthplace Museum ends 'W.N. next', an ordering not reflected in any list. Many sketches have more than one proposed location indicated, usually a roman numeral in pencil and Arabic in blue pencil; for instance, this moves R.P.A. from XI to 5, 'Ysobel' from XII to 6, 'Nimrod' from VIII to 9, and B.G.N. from IV or V to 12. Some of these locations are not proposed on any of the lists as I have interpreted them.

5 The enigmas

1 'Elgar's humour', Reed, *Elgar*, p. 53; Burley, p. 120; a 'leg-pull' (Ernest Newman, 'Elgar and his Variations: What was the Enigma?', *Sunday Times*, 16, 23 and 30 April and 7 May 1939, cited in Kennedy, *Portrait*, p. 96); a 'jape' (Elgar's favourite term: Young, *Elgar O.M.*, p. 279).

2 Richard Powell, 'Elgar's Enigma', *Music and Letters* 15 (1934), pp. 203–6, reprinted in Redwood (ed.), *Companion*, pp. 50–5; Roger Fiske, 'The Enigma – a Solution', *The Musical Times* 110 (1969), pp. 1124–6, reprinted in Redwood, pp. 76–81. Only Jaeger and Alice, who both predeceased Elgar, may have known his own solution.

3 Maine, *Elgar* I, p. 271.

4 The note is by C. Barry, quoting an untraced letter from Elgar.

5 Theodore van Houten takes it to be the future tense (strictly 'I shall'): '"You of All People": Elgar's *Enigma*', *The Music Review* 37 (1976), pp. 130–42. David Crystal in *The Cambridge Encyclopaedia of the English Language* (Cambridge University Press, 1995, p. 224) says that 'modern usage does not observe the distinction', but this is too categorical even for today, and certainly for 1899.

6 The Maeterlinck reference is a characteristic show of literary culture. Both plays relate to dying women who are never on stage; Death, 'the intruder' in the first-named play, is not the absent protagonist (as claimed by Moore, *Creative Life*, p. 270); Trowell, 'Literature', pp. 216–17.

7 Powell, *Memories*, pp. 119, 121, reiterated in *The Musical Times* 80 (1939), p. 60 ('Elgar told me personally more than once that the enigma concerned another tune'); but she perhaps inconsistently said 'we always spoke of the hidden matter as "it", never as tune or theme' (*Memories*, p. 119).

8 Powell, *Memories*, p. 23. She was supported in her belief that a tune was integral to the solution by Winifred Norbury and Elgar's daughter Carice (writing in 1942; in October 1898 Carice was eight). On Griffith's observations concerning interpretation as a ballet, see Young, *Elgar O.M.*, p. 278.

9 'The "dark saying" seems not to be posed as a puzzle with a clear and simple solution such as many speculators have attempted to suggest for it.' *Complete Edition*, p. v.

10 Note for the Aeolian 'Duo-Art' pianola rolls, a section not reproduced in *MFPW*. See Kennedy, *Portrait*, p. 91, and *Complete Edition*, p. x. As Geoffrey Poole notes, the sequential sevenths are not peculiarly Elgarian ('Questioning the Enigma', *Music and Musicians* (August 1971), p. 29).

11 Gordon Lee, 'Another Piece in the Jigsaw', makes a helpful tabulation of solutions (pp. 254–5) and Rollett, 'New Light', surveys much of the prior literature. There are doubtless more 'solutions', including many that are unpublished.

12 Young, *Elgar O.M.*, pp. 280, 385 (music examples).

13 Trowell, 'Literature', p. 312.

14 Rollett, 'New Light', p. 114. The melody is not doubled in thirds, is in compound time, and rises to a mediant rather than supertonic climax; moreover, it needs to be transposed.

15 Westrup, 'Elgar's Enigma', p. 96.

16 Stanford's melody shares the general contour of the first bar of theme A, but the last interval is a diminished fifth, not a third (a–f–b♭–e), and his second bar is an exact sequence: these are not trivial differences. His tune, however, also starts off the beat. This connection was noted by Raymond Leppard in *The Times*, 20 August 1977.

17 Skouenborg brackets the pitches E♭–D (up to) B♭–G, although the theme contains no E♭s: 'Elgar's *Enigma*: The Solution', *The Music Review* 43 (1982), pp. 161–8: see p. 167.

18 Ben Kingdon, 'The "Enigma" – a Hidden "Dark Saying" ', *Elgar Society Journal* 1 (May 1979), pp. 9–12. The third phrase of the chant roughly fits theme B; but the second phrase, emerging simultaneously with the first from theme A, has to share several of the same notes. He also mentions 'Home, sweet home' if played in B♭ major (see appendix).

19 See above, p. 46; Westrup, 'Elgar's Enigma', pp. 93–4; Parrott, *Elgar*, p. 42.

20 Thomas Arne set the word 'never' only once, 'ne-' being slurred over five notes: *Alfred*, in *Musica Britannica* xlvii (London: Stainer and Bell, 1981), p. 148; van Houten, ' "You of All People" ', p. 133.

21 The idea was anticipated in the *Daily Telegraph* (26 March 1977); see Denis Stevens, letter to *The Musical Times* 133 (1992), p. 62, supporting the van Houten 'solution'. Moore, 'The Enigma Solution', *Sunday Telegraph*, 3 November 1991. Previously Moore had suggested Elgar was playing reminiscently through *Caractacus* (*Creative Life*, p. 248), but the themes he quotes are not, as he implies, in G.

22 See p. 46. On 11 November 1898 he wrote to Jaeger: 'as to Gordon, the thing possesses me, but I can't write it down yet': Moore, *Publishers*, p. 96.

23 The transposition may be considered a weakness if we agree with Young (*Elgar O.M.*, p. 279), Parrott (see Redwood (ed.), *Companion*, pp. 88–9), and Moore (*Creative Life*, pp. 248–9) on the importance to Elgar of the parallel modes of G. However, Trowell identifies an early sketch in E minor which may tenuously be related to the final version as 'Lml's' (it appears upside-down within the British Library sketch collection): 'Literature', p. 220 and note 147 (pp. 306–7).

24 Jaeger's letter, of 7 November 1899, was written at the time when Elgar might well have divulged something about the secret behind the 'enigma': Trowell, 'Literature', p. 307; see Moore, *Publishers*, p. 148, and Powell, *Memories*, p. 28. While usually signing his letters 'Ed. Elgar' or 'Ed. E.', the composer signed a published letter with a clef and the note E: *The Musical Times* 38 (1897), p. 741.

103

25 On the Tasso line, see Trowell's thorough review of the evidence: 'Literature', pp. 213–15.

26 Sams supplies a list of parallels between Elgar and Schumann: 'Variations on an Original Theme (Enigma)', p. 261. His evidence on Schumann's ciphers had appeared in *The Musical Times* in 1965–6. His more recent article 'Elgar's Enigmas' (*Music and Letters* 78 (1997), pp. 410–15) does not concern Op. 36.

27 The third bar contains the notes D, G, B♭, and A, the first four notes of *Auld lang syne* played in the minor mode. See Sams, 'Variations on an Original Theme (Enigma)', p. 258.

28 Sams, 'Elgar's Cipher Letter to Dorabella', *The Musical Times* 111 (1970), pp. 151–4.

29 Parrott has developed his ideas in *Elgar*, pp. 46–9; 'Elgar's Two-fold Enigma: A Religious Sequel', *Music and Letters* 54 (1973), pp. 57–60; and in Redwood (ed.), *Companion*, pp. 82–90.

30 Marshall A. Portnoy, 'The Answer to Elgar's *Enigma*', *The Musical Quarterly* 71 (1985), pp. 205–10. The argument depends on the number 43, on the basis A=1, B=2 being the numerical equivalent of J. S. Bach (with initials) and Elgar (without). But no 'solution' is credible which identifies forty-three notes in the 'first-violin statement of the main theme' (bars 1–10, a line much of which is not the theme at all), depends on an imagined resemblance between Elgar's theme and the BACH motive, and identifies bars 8–10 as a 'three-measure coda'.

31 Poole, 'Questioning the Enigma', pp. 26–9. That 'Caroline' is incomplete and 'Alice' an anagram is attributed to the intervention of technique following a literal but musically unsatisfactory encoding of the name.

32 Christopher Seaman, note to his recording of *Variations* with the National Youth Orchestra, PCD 1080 (1994).

33 David Vaughan, *Frederick Ashton and his Ballets* (London: Adam and Charles Black, 1977), p. 363.

34 See Kennedy, *Portrait*, pp. 85–6; Powell, *Memories*, p. 38 (with facsimile); Moore, *Letters of a Lifetime*, p. 102. As it is contrasted with the 'nice' 'Dorabella' motive, Poole suggests the unideal was an allusion to Alice ('Questioning the Enigma', p. 28). But Dora was drawn from Alice's social world and such disloyalty seems unlikely.

35 Trowell, 'Literature', p. 312. The *Caractacus* fugue is in C minor, the answer in G minor.

36 Theme A has to be in G major for this purpose. See Rollett, 'New Light', pp. 111 (admitting the poor fit in bars 3–4 of the theme if the harmonies are included) and 118.

37 Charles Ross, 'A Key to the Enigma', *Elgar Society Journal* 8 (September 1994), pp. 265–9.

38 Westrup, 'Elgar's Enigma', pp. 91–2; Poole, 'Questioning the Enigma', pp. 27–8. Arguments against the existence of another tune are effectively countered by Rollett, 'New Light', pp. 109–10.

39 *The Musical Times* 38 (1897), p. 741; reprinted in their profile of Elgar, *The Musical Times* 41 (1900), p. 647, which is in turn reprinted in vol. 139 (February 1998), p. 22. See Moore, *Publishers*, p. 53.

40 *The Musical Times* 41 (1900), p. 647; Buckley, *Sir Edward Elgar*, pp. 54–5. Poole ('Questioning the Enigma') argues that Elgar never confirmed this wording, but nor did he deny it. Dora Powell supported Buckley's claim that his biography was authorised: *Memories*, p. 120.

41 Richard Powell, 'Elgar's Enigma'.

42 McVeagh, *Edward Elgar*, p. 26.

43 A. H. Fox Strangways in *Music and Letters* 15 (1934), pp. 207–8, reprinted in Redwood (ed.), *Companion*, pp. 54–5.

44 See Redwood (ed.), *Companion*, p. 81. Accepting bar 4, at which some had jibbed, Fox Strangways queried the counterpoint of bar 9, and objected to the consecutives: *Music and Letters* 16 (1935), pp. 37–9, reprinted in Redwood (ed.), *Companion*, pp. 56–9.

45 His claim that the whole tune can finally be heard against the last peroration in the finale, however, depends on counterpoint more suited to Ives or Grainger than Elgar: Derek Hudson, 'Elgar's Enigma: the Trail of the Evidence', *The Musical Times* 125 (1984), pp. 636–9.

46 The *Dies Irae* as cantus firmus (Kenneth Kemsey-Bourne, 'The Real Answer to Elgar's Riddle', *Elgar Society Journal* 4 (September 1986), pp. 9–12) is a particularly bad fit, and further derivations where the first four notes of the chant are permutated into a simple scale amount to Baconian reasoning which could lead anywhere, including *Heart of Oak*. Skouenborg essays a crude bass to the second of Brahms's *Serious Songs* (published 1896), using A in altered rhythmic values (Elgar altered the National Anthem to combine with Tchaikovsky's melody, see note 39), and a truly awful counterpoint of the fourth song with 'Nimrod' ('Elgar's *Enigma*', pp. 163–4). Despite the consecutive fifths in the theme (bar 6), Elgar's contrapuntal 'japes' have vigour and work: see the 'moral coda' to *Cockaigne* combining the love theme with Mendelssohn's Wedding March over the 'Troyte' ostinato (Young, *Elgar O.M.*, facing p. 161).

47 Tovey, 'Elgar, Master of Music', *Music and Letters* 16 (1935), p. 4.

48 Powell, *Memories*, p. 120 and *The Musical Times* 80 (1939), p. 60. Young suggests that *inter alia Variations* embodies 'the spirit of Malvern': 'Friends', p. 85.

49 Young, *Elgar O.M.*, p. 278. An analogy is suggested by Diana McVeagh with *Falstaff* which, as Elgar wrote to Ernest Newman, 'is the name but Shakespeare – the whole of human life – is the theme': 'Elgar and *Falstaff*' in Monk (ed.), *Elgar Studies*, p. 134; Moore, *Letters of a Lifetime*, p. 263.

50 This connection was noticed by Mrs Cecil Dickenson in 1939 and developed by Diana McVeagh, *Edward Elgar*, p. 26. It receives support from Sams, 'Variations', p. 262, and Rollett, 'New Light', p. 122.

51 Elgar attended mass on 12 February 1899, when the passage from Corinthians (in Latin) was the epistle. One of the Brahms *Serious Songs* sets these words of St Paul.

52 Moore, 'An Approach to Elgar's "Enigma" ', pp. 38–44 (see p. 38). See also Moore, *Creative Life*, pp. 259–66; Westrup, 'Elgar's Enigma', pp. 81 ff. Skouenborg relates the enigma to Elgar's moral weakness, self-pity, 'Elgar's *Enigma*', p. 167.

53 Rollett, 'New Light', pp. 121 ff. Michael Hurd (*Elgar*, London: Faber, 1969) and Michael Kennedy (*Portrait*) are cited in support of this autobiographical trajectory; Burley (p. 117) also associated the theme with Elgar's 'loneliness as an artist'.

54 Rainer Fanselau, *Die Orgel im Werk Edward Elgars* (*Göttinger Musikwissenschaftliche Arbeiten* 5, Göttingen: Andreas Funke, 1973), pp. 290–3. In addition Fanselau suggests that the organ confirms *Variations* as a sign of a patriotic, Victorian, and conservative world-view.

55 Trowell, 'Literature', p. 215, referring to the 'almost military determination' of E.D.U.

56 Burley, p. 131. On Elgar's frequent claims about hostility and discouragement, see the prelude to Kennedy, *Portrait*, p. 15.

57 Westrup implies that Sinclair's challenge to set Dan's adventure to music must have been met immediately, in the summer of 1898, and the material adapted for the theme ('Elgar's Enigma', p. 96). But the incident may have occurred in late October (Moore, *Creative Life*, p. 254, and *Complete Edition*, p. vii).

58 Parrott compares it to a specific G minor pedal exercise (Redwood (ed.), *Companion*, p. 83). As with 'Ysobel', Elgar has written in a difficulty (not in the Bach); at this tempo, the first three notes of 47:3 are awkward since the player cannot simply use alternate feet.

59 Moore, *Creative Life*, p. 264; on this point, see Trowell, 'Literature', pp. 220–1.

60 Letter of 25 July 1899: 'The variations (especially *** no. 13) have been a great triumph...' Cited by Young, 'Friends', p. 95; Moore, *Publishers*, p. 117.

61 Burley, pp. 125–6; Newman, letter to Alice Stuart-Wortley's daughter, cited in Kennedy, *Portrait*, p. 97.

62 Kennedy, *Portrait*, first edition, pp. 67–9, without naming Weaver; second edition, pp. 95–8; the third edition provides additional information, pp. 31–2. See also Trowell, 'Literature', pp. 217–24, and the book by her relation, the local historian Cora Weaver, confusedly entitled *The 13th Enigma?* (London: Thames, 1988).

63 Atkins, *The Elgar–Atkins Friendship*, pp. 477–80. Burley's suggestion (p. 126) that the subject would have known of the dedication might be counted against Weaver.

64 Burley, pp. 125–6. Alternative sources for the three-note quotation are easy to find: Beethoven (*Fidelio* or – particularly appropriate – *Les Adieux* Op. 81a, both with different rhythms); Schumann (Piano Concerto, in the minor, like the trombone version (cue 58) which is *not* in quotes); Berlioz (*Benvenuto Cellini*, ending the romance 'La gloire était ma seule idole' with 'Protect her, protect me'); even the sea-swept *Flying Dutchman*. But Gordon Lee ('Another Piece in the Jigsaw', pp. 63–4) relates the quotation to Mendelssohn's Wedding March (*A Midsummer Night's Dream*).

65 Nicholas Reed tried to rule out both Lygon and Weaver, whom he believed had died in 1885 (she emigrated to New Zealand in October 1885 and died in 1927), and names Julia Worthington as (***), although offering no evidence that Elgar met her before 1903: 'Elgar's Enigmatic Inamorata', *The Musical Times* 125 (August 1984), pp. 430–4.

66 See the first of the poems transcribed by Trowell, 'Literature', p. 298.

67 The evidence of the sketches is conclusive; see Trowell, 'Literature', pp. 219–22, for a résumé of this problem, in which he suggests that Lygon, whom Elgar called 'angelic', may have been his confidante concerning Helen Weaver.

68 Douglas Jarman, 'Secret Programmes', in Anthony Pople (ed.), *The Cambridge Companion to Berg* (Cambridge University Press, 1997), pp. 167–79.

69 Unlike Brian Newbould's solution to a cryptic remark Elgar made about his String Quartet: '"Never Done Before": Elgar's Other Enigma', *Music and Letters* 77 (1996), pp. 228–41.

70 The exercise GBECBDCAG, with the pairs exchanged: *Music and Letters* 44 (1963), p. 98. Van Houten overplays his hand by fitting citations from Alexander Pope's *Epistle to Dr Arbuthnot* to each variation; some (notably the composer) fit the cap, but others seem forced, even trivial: '"You of All People"', pp. 135–42.

71 Brian Trowell tells me that he is working on a fuller solution for future publication.

6 Postscript

1 Bernard Herrmann, 'An American Voice', in H. A. Chambers (ed.), *Edward Elgar Centenary Sketches* (London: Novello, 1957), pp. 17–18.

2 *The Musical Times* 40 (July 1899), pp. 464, 471.

3 *The Musical Times* 40 (November 1899), p. 757; advertisement, 41 (1900), p. 71.

4 Michael Kennedy, 'Some Elgar Interpreters', in Monk (ed.), *Elgar Studies*, pp. 221–36 (cited p. 223). The ensuing discussion is much indebted to this admirable study, and to Robert Philip, *Early Recordings and Musical Style* (on Op. 36, see pp. 28, 36, 81–2, 183–4, 187, 190, 234).

5 Recordings discussed: 1926, Royal Albert Hall Orchestra/Elgar, reissue on LP, World Record Club, SH 162; 1935, BBC Symphony Orchestra/ Toscanini, live performance, CDH 769784-2; 1954, Royal Philharmonic Orchestra/Beecham, Philips ABl 3053; 1955, Hallé Orchestra/Barbirolli, reissued on CD, EMI CDM 7 63955 2, giving the date as 1957; 1961, London Philharmonic Orchestra/Boult, World Record Club T 158; Philadelphia Orchestra/Ormandy, CBS 72982; 1974, Chicago Symphony Orchestra/ Solti, London 425 155–2. Generalisations are based on a much wider sampling, including living conductors.

6 Powell, *Memories*, p. 106.

7 Kennedy says that Harty's 1932 recording was 'the last time on record that "Nimrod" has no overtones of the Cenotaph': 'Some Elgar Interpreters', p. 230.

8 Ibid., p. 225; Philip, *Early Recordings*, p. 184.

9 Philip, *Early Recordings*, p. 240.

10 Elgar writes in a letter to Jaeger (28 May 1899): 'Another "Enigma" – the Black Knight you say is unsuccessful commercially . . .' There is no identification of a first enigma, which suggests the question must already have been discussed; however, the end of the letter is missing: Moore, *Publishers*, p. 124.

11 Reed, *Elgar*, p. 53; Herrmann, 'An American Voice', p. 19; personal communication from Geoffrey Poole. Bar 1 could equally well be sung to Alice Elgar; Carice Elgar; Hubert Leicester; Dorabella; Rosa Burley; Helen Weaver; Peter Gurney; Peter Davey . . . but I do not propose *Widdecombe Fair* as a solution.

12 For a thoughtful review of the question of musical portraiture, based on *Variations*, see Sparshott, 'Portraits in Music – A Case-Study'.

13 On the rhetoric of musical character see Richard Greene, *Holst: The Planets* (Cambridge University Press, 1995), pp. 4–8.

14 Buckley, *Sir Edward Elgar*, p. 32.

15 Violin Sonata, two before fig. 54, accented in the piano right hand. I am indebted to Brian Trowell for drawing this to my attention.

16 Eric-Emmanuel Schmitt, *Variations énigmatiques*, a one-act play performed in Paris in 1996: my translation (from the German translation).

17 Sams, 'Variations on an Original Theme (Enigma)', p. 261.

Select bibliography

Anderson, Robert. *Elgar in Manuscript* (London: The British Library, 1990)
  Elgar ('The Master Musicians', London: Dent, 1993)
Atkins, E. Wulstan. *The Elgar–Atkins Friendship* (Newton Abbot: David and
  Charles, 1984)
Buckley, R. J. *Sir Edward Elgar* ('Living Masters of Music', London: John Lane.
  The Bodley Head, 1905)
Burley, Rosa and Carruthers, Frank C. *Edward Elgar: The Record of a Friendship*
  (London: Barrie and Jenkins, 1972)
Craggs, Stewart. *Edward Elgar. A Source Book* (Aldershot: Scolar Press, 1995)
Del Mar, Norman. *Conducting Elgar* (Oxford: Clarendon Press, 1998)
Dibble, Jeremy. *C. Hubert H. Parry: His Life and Music* (Oxford University
  Press, 1992)
Elgar, Edward. *My Friends Pictured Within. The Subjects of the Enigma Variations
  as Portrayed in Contemporary Photographs and Elgar's Manuscript* (Seven-
  oaks: Novello, n.d. [1946], republication of notes for Aeolian Company's
  piano rolls, 1929)
  A Future for English Music and Other Lectures (ed. Percy M. Young; London:
  Dennis Dobson, 1968)
Fifield, Christopher. *True Artist and True Friend: A Biography of Hans Richter*
  (Oxford: Clarendon Press, 1993)
Kennedy, Michael. *Portrait of Elgar* (Oxford University Press, 1968; second
  edition 1982; third edition, Clarendon Paperback, 1987)
  Elgar Orchestral Music (London: BBC Music Guide, 1973)
Kent, Christopher. *Edward Elgar: A Guide to Research* (New York: Garland,
  1993)
Lee, Gordon. 'Another Piece in the Jigsaw', *Elgar Society Journal* 8 (September
  1994), pp. 252–65
Maine, Basil. *Elgar, his Life and Works.* Vol. I (Life), vol. II (Works) (London: G.
  Bell & Sons, 1933)
McVeagh, Diana. *Edward Elgar: His Life and Music* (London: Dent, 1955)

Monk, Raymond (ed.). *Elgar Studies* (Aldershot: Scolar Press, 1990)

(ed.). *Edward Elgar: Music and Literature* (Aldershot: Scolar Press, 1993)

Moore, Jerrold Northrop. 'An Approach to Elgar's "Enigma"', *The Music Review* 20 (1959), pp. 38–44

Edward Elgar: A Creative Life (Oxford University Press, 1984)

Elgar and his Publishers: Letters of a Creative Life. 2 vols. (Oxford University Press, 1987)

Edward Elgar: Letters of a Lifetime (Oxford University Press, 1990)

Newman, Ernest. *Elgar* (London: John Lane. The Bodley Head, 1906)

Parrott, Ian. *Elgar* ('The Master Musicians', London: Dent, 1971)

Philip, Robert. *Early Recordings and Musical Style* (Cambridge University Press, 1992)

Powell, Mrs Richard [Dora Penny]. *Edward Elgar: Memories of a Variation* (London: Oxford University Press, 1937; third, enlarged, edition, London: Methuen, 1949)

Redwood, Christopher (ed.). *An Elgar Companion* (Ashbourne: Sequoia Publishing, 1982)

Reed, William. *Elgar as I Knew Him* (London: Gollancz, 1938, reissued 1973)

Elgar ('The Master Musicians', London: Dent, 1939; third edition rev. Eric Blom, 1949)

Rollett, J. M. 'New Light on Elgar's Enigma', *Elgar Society Journal* 10 (November 1997), pp. 106–23

Sams, Eric. 'Variations on an Original Theme (Enigma)', *The Musical Times* 111 (1970), pp. 258–62

Shera, F. H. *Elgar: Instrumental Works* I ('The Musical Pilgrim', London: Oxford University Press, 1931)

Sparshott, Francis. 'Portraits in Music – A Case-Study: Elgar's "Enigma" Variations', in M. Kreusz (ed.), *The Interpretation of Music: Philosophical Essays* (Oxford: Clarendon Press, 1993)

Tovey, D. F. 'Variations for Orchestra, Op. 36', in *Essays in Musical Analysis* IV (Illustrative Music) (London: Oxford University Press, 1935), pp. 149–52, reprinted in *Symphonies and Other Orchestral Works* (London: Oxford University Press, 1981), pp. 317–20

Trowell, Brian. 'Elgar's Use of Literature', in Monk (ed.), *Edward Elgar: Music and Literature*, pp. 182–326

Westrup, J. A. 'Elgar's Enigma', *Proceedings of the Royal Musical Association* 86 (1959–60), pp. 79–97

Young, Percy M. *Elgar O.M. A Study of a Musician* (London: Collins, 1955)

'Friends Pictured Within', in Monk (ed.), *Elgar Studies*, pp. 81–106

Index

112

Index

113

Index

114